BUSINESS HISTORY:
CONCEPTS AND MEASUREMENT

BUSINESS HISTORY
CONCEPTS AND MEASUREMENT

Edited by
CHARLES HARVEY

Routledge
Taylor & Francis Group

LONDON AND NEW YORK

First published 1989 by
FRANK CASS AND COMPANY LIMITED
Published 2013 by Routledge

and in the United States of America by
Routledge
2 Park Square, Milton Park, Abingdon, Oxfordshire OX14 4RN
711 Third Avenue, New York, NY 10017

First issued in paperback 2014

Routledge is an imprint of the Taylor & Francis Group, an informa business

Copyright © 1989 Frank Cass & Co. Ltd.

British Library Cataloguing in Publication Data

Business history: concepts and measurement.
1. Great Britain. Industrialisation. Social aspects,
history
I. Harvey, Charles, *1950–*
303.4'83'0941

ISBN 978-0-714-63366-4 (hbk)
ISBN 978-0-415-76120-8 (pbk)

Library of Congress Cataloging-in-publication Data

Business history : concepts and measurement / edited by Charles
Harvey.
    p.   cm.
    "This group of studies first appeared in a special issue on Business
history: Concepts and measurements of Business history, vol. 31, no. 3"
—CIP t.p. verso.
    Includes index.
    ISBN 0-7146-3366-6
    1. Great Britain—Industries—History.   2. Business enterprises—
Great Britain—History.   I. Harvey, Charles, 1950– .
HC255.B87 1989
338.0941–dc20   89-9698
                                                                  CIP

This group of studies first appeared in a Special Issue of *Business
History*, Vol.XXXI, No.3. (July 1989), [Business History: Concepts
and Measurement].

CONTENTS

BUSINESS HISTORY:
CONCEPTS AND MEASUREMENT

By CHARLES HARVEY

The decade of the 1960s was one of great intellectual achievement for economic history. It witnessed the flowering of the new economic history, the results of which have made a deep and lasting impact on many fields of enquiry – the economics of slavery, the contribution of railways to economic development, the causes of industrialisation in the United States, and the issue of technological choice in nineteenth-century Britain are examples that spring to mind.[1] The extra charge to the subject supplied through the application of cliometric methods, moreover, has not been lost. By no means all economic historians would identify themselves wholeheartedly with the cause of the new economic history, but few would deny that the standards of reasoning and evidence set in the 1960s have helped to raise the general quality of argument and research. Yet, curiously, the methods of the new economic history have had but little impact on business history. The specialist journals – *Business History* and *Business History Review* – carry few articles which draw extensively on economic theory or employ advanced statistical methods.

There is no simple explanation for this. It may be that the majority of business historians simply lacks the expertise needed to make effective use of theory or quantification. Equally, many business historians would deny the relevance of most economic ideas or techniques of measurement to their work. Close studies of individual firms until recently have been the favoured topics for research, and it is fair to say that neo-classical economics has little to offer those concerned with the minutiae of organisation, management and policy-making. Traditional theories of the firm thus might be held up as unrealistic, irrelevant to the realities of business life. And since cliometrics was in the early years closely identified with neo-classicism, it could be argued that the business historian might well find the whole approach intellectually bankrupt. Certainly, the business history community, whilst taking note of the ideas of alternative theorists of the firm like Edith Penrose,[2] has generally regarded economic theory with suspicion, preferring the research methods of traditional history to those those of social science.

Faced with a problem or unexplained issue, the first impulse of the traditionally-minded historian is to seek illumination through a detailed examination of the available documentary record. Primary research is all important. Sources stimulate ideas and the referencing of similar cases. The result of the research process is an interpretation of a source or set of sources; generalisation is the product of comparisons between cases. The approach might be described as source-driven, although there is a continuous interplay between ideas and evidence. It is in this manner that scores of company history monographs have been compiled to form the core of the existing literature of business history. Few studies involve extensive quantification, since the emphasis is squarely on the particular rather that than the general. Indeed, many business historians seem unaware that statistical techniques, however simple, are nowadays routinely applied in many branches of historical research. One result, stemming ultimately from the narrow intellectual focus of the subject, is the frequent abuse of words like 'significant', 'rapid' and 'typical'. All too often generalisation is attempted on the basis of a handful of non-systematic case studies.

The fact that so many works of business history lack a sound quantitative foundation is not a consequence of the dominance of the source-driven approach to historical research. Neither quantification nor computing are inimical to traditional research practices. Economic historians of all sorts – from the most traditional to the most social scientific – have for long been concerned with the construction and analysis of series of data that describe aspects of economic change; notably series for population, production, employment, trade and investment. Accurate measurement is accepted as a precondition for meaningful historical analysis, and what is true of economic history must be true for its sub-discipline, business history. Three of the essays presented in this volume illustrate this point. The articles by Church, Moss and Morgan, and Shaw are based on traditional forms of research, yet each, through the use of relatively simple statistical measures, makes an important contribution to the subject under consideration. Church presents detailed estimates for production, employment and labour productivity in the British coalfields, 1830–1913, which point to the need to revise previous judgements on the development and performance of the industry. Moss and Morgan make innovative use of the financial records of a Scottish shipbuilder in exploring the dynamics of wealth creation and distribution. Most previous studies of the distribution of wealth have been based on the valuation of estates at the time of death; the essay highlights the limitation of this approach and presents an alternative which promises to yield rich insights into Victorian business behaviour and morality. Likewise Shaw takes a more rigorous look at the origins, education, training and careers of British business leaders than hitherto has been possible. Her analysis is based on data relating to 375 businessmen chronicled in the multi-volume *Dictionary of Business Biography*.[3] Entrepreneurs in steel (73) and distribution (114) are compared with a random sample of 188 subjects from all other sectors covered in the dictionary.

Three of the studies in this volume, by Foreman-Peck, Treble, and Hudson, are of a very different character to the three outlined above. The application of economic theory and advanced techniques of measurement, in different combinations, is their hallmark. They are examples of social scientific history, in the fashion of the new economic history. Rather than looking straightaway at the available documentary evidence, the first procedure of the 'new business historian' is to explore a subject in theoretical terms. The aim is the construction of a model which identifies a set of system variables and the manner in which they are related. Models are logical constructions which describe the workings of an economic system, or, more usually, an economic sub-system. The researcher is free to derive a model from any relevant body of theory, and to limit its scope and level of complexity. In historical research, the purpose of the model is to provide an intellectually coherent account of the workings of the system or institution under examination. This is made plain in Treble's incisive essay on the operation of the coal industry conciliation boards, 1893–1914. In this the author refutes the notion that systematic differences in the ways in which area boards reached decisions can be explained in terms of personalities, pointing instead to the importance of fundamental differences in the rules which governed their actions. Treble 'takes it as read' that in modelling the behaviour of management and labour board representatives 'the appropriate techniques are those of game theory, which now forms the basis of economists' thinking in issues about bargaining and arbitration'.[4]

Once a preliminary model has been formulated the next stage in the research process is to test it against the historical evidence. This frequently but not always involves the use of advanced measurement and estimation techniques. Whatever the case, the aim is to ascertain the explanatory power and robustness of the model. It may either be judged to fit the facts well or to be lacking in some way. If the latter is the case, the model either can be rejected or refined and re-tested. The modelling–testing cycle may be repeated until the researcher is satisfied with the model or is defeated by the complexities of reality. Foreman-Peck and Hudson each make use of multiple regression methods in their work, indicating the importance and generality of the technique. Regression models are conceptually simple, positing that the value of one variable in a system (the dependent variable with which the researcher is especially concerned) is determined by the values of the other (independent) variables in the system. Regression equations are estimated to find the precise form of the relationship between dependent and independent variables, revealing which of the latter have the strongest influence over the former. The degree to which variations in a dependent variable can be explained by corresponding variations in related independent variables gives a measure (the R^2 statistic) of the explanatory power of a model. Although regression models are simple to understand, experience is an advantage when interpreting the results of an estimation.

Both Foreman-Peck and Hudson use regression analysis to good effect, adopting the standard models-analysis form of presentation. Foreman-Peck is concerned with the efficiency of the British telegraph system in the nineteenth century, under private management and subsequently as a nationalised industry. He examines industry costs, competition and technological progress. He concludes that neither the private nor nationalised industries performed ideally, and that regulated private monopoly may have been a better organisational form. Yet there is insufficient evidence to conclude that the British system performed badly by international standards. Hudson is concerned with the relatively high birth and low death rates of British limited liability companies in the 1930s. He identifies rising profitability, declining real interest rates, high unemployment and the introduction of tariffs in 1932 as key explanatory variables, arguing that 'the depression carried the seeds of self correction, with a semi-automatic shift towards a more entrepreneurial, small firm, based economy'.[5] The findings of both authors are persuasive, not least because of the judicious balance struck between economic logic and statistical interpretation in the presentation of arguments.

The final essay in the collection, that of Nicholas on the international distribution of British-based manufacturing plants, cannot readily be classified as either specifically historical or social scientific in construction. The author argues that allegations that the overseas plants of British multinationals performed badly before 1939, causing a defensive retreat to Empire, cannot be sustained on the basis of a selective reading of a handful of case studies. His position is that all business historians, whatever their research technique, should be systematic in approach and conceptually aware. He explains the importance of transactions costs economics to business history generally, and more particularly to the study of foreign direct investment. In the light of the theory, the international distribution of the foreign plants of a sample of 448 pre-1939 manufacturing multinationals is detailed and explained with reference both to a formal model and case study evidence. The two research techniques are seen as complementary.

It is hoped that this collection of studies, embracing a number of concepts, methods and approaches to business history research, will encourage other scholars to consider the range of possibilities open to them. There are advantages to the source-driven approach to historical enquiry, notably in the stimulation of the historical imagination. But these advantages are lost without the reference points resulting from accurate measurement. Much can still be achieved through the systematic application in history of relatively simple statistical techniques. The alternative methods of the 'new business historian' will not appeal to all researchers. Yet, as the essays in this volume demonstrate, to deny the power of economic logic would be folly. Concepts as well as facts can stimulate the open mind.

Royal Holloway & Bedford New College, London

NOTES

1. The term 'new economic history' first became common currency in the early 1960s. Richard Sutch attributes it to D.C. North. See R.L. Ransom *et al., Explorations in the New Economic History* (New York, 1982), p.22. A clear explanation of new economic history aims and methods is given by R.W. Fogel, 'The New Economic History, Its Findings and Methods', in D. Rowney and J. Graham, *Quantitative History* (Homewood, Il, 1969).
2. E. Penrose, *The Theory of the Growth of the Firm* (1959).
3. D.J. Jeremy and C. Shaw (eds.), *Dictionary of Business Biography*, 5 vols. (London, 1984–86).
4. See below, p.65.
5. See below, p.119.

PRODUCTION, EMPLOYMENT AND LABOUR PRODUCTIVITY IN THE BRITISH COALFIELDS, 1830–1913: SOME REINTERPRETATIONS

By ROY CHURCH

The analysis and interpretation of the origins and course of British industrialisation has taken a new turn. Hitherto historians have emphasised the strategic role of leading *manufacturing* sectors which produced goods possessing high value added. In recent years attention has switched to a model of the economy in which a highly productive agricultural sector is seen as a crucial enabling factor in the early stages of industrialisation, and in which Britain's favourable mineral endowment, particularly coal, permitted an elasticity of supply conspicuously lacking on the continent of Europe, where industrial progress was hampered as a result.[1] Like agriculture, the coal industry relied overwhelmingly upon unskilled labour, but coal was much more than an enabling factor, a passive industry merely responding to a growing demand for its output. The concentration of capital, technical expertise and managerial know-how produced an industrial dynamism in the coal industry which created the steam engine and the railways, which not only transformed the coal industry but also laid the foundations of Britain's mid-nineteenth century comparative advantage in manufacturing.[2] Britain dominated the international trade in coal for the remainder of the century; in 1913 only cotton exceeded coal in export value – and many of Britain's imports were cheaper as a result.[3] During the long Victorian boom coal was the pivot upon which British pre-eminence rested.

Prefacing his improvement of the estimates of coal output during the industrial revolution, in 1980 Pollard asserted that the geography and technology of industrial Britain 'were clearly influenced by coal and possibly even dictated by it'.[4] Stressing that the flow of resources into the industry represented one of the strongest growth elements in the economy, he concluded that timing and location should be among the key variables in any detailed study of Britain's industrialisation, and that a necessary condition for explaining them was a reliable production series. Such a series not only enables us to chart the growth in productive capacity, but provides a basis for estimating capital formation and the growth and fluctuations of investment. All recent capital estimates for the industry are derived from capital–output ratios employed as multipliers applied to production, consequently the reliability of the series presented by Mitchell, Pollard and Feinstein rest upon the accuracy of the output estimates on which they were based;[5] our revised output estimates, therefore, invalidate existing series for capital formation in the nineteenth century. Reliable employment series are equally necessary not only to chart the expansion of the workforce, but to obtain a measure of labour productivity defined as output per man year (OMY).

The effect of the various revisions made to coal's key statistics published between 1978 and 1984 was broadly to confirm the long-established view of the industry: that rapidly rising productivity during the mid-nineteenth century was followed by decline from the 1880s. Mitchell's production series for 1800–1914 (incorporating Pollard's new estimates to 1850) revealed a deceleration in annual rates of growth, which Mitchell interpreted as 'evidence of a clear watershed … in the early 1870s'.[6] Trends in output per man year and per man shift (OMS) were shown to have reached their turning point in the 1880s, from which time, according to Mitchell, 'the efficiency of British coalmining was declining'.[7] This amounts to an endorsement of the traditional view, first expressed by Clapham and subsequently reinforced in the 1960s by Taylor's important research into the industry's performance.[8] The serious consequences for the rest of the economy were underlined by Matthews, Feinstein and Odling Smee, whose calculations of total factor productivity implied a record worse than that for any other sector,[9] while econometric historians are engaged in animated debate in search for explanations for declining labour productivity.[10]

Following the appearance of Pollard's 1980 series, and coincident with the presentation of Mitchell's 1984 series, another set of production, employment, capital and productivity estimates were in preparation, and for the first time may now be compared.[11] The new estimates reveal important differences, both at national and regional levels, and in contrast to previous accounts of the industry prompt the following conclusions: that annual rates of growth in production began to decline shortly after the mid-century; that the rate of growth in output was broadly constant between the early 1870s and 1913; that labour productivity (OMY and OMS) rose modestly rather than dramatically during the early and mid-Victorian boom in coal production between the 1830s and the 1870s; and that the decline in OMY and OMS in the Edwardian erea was largely a consequence of the Eight Hours Act – and therefore cannot be interpreted as a failure either of the industry's entrepreneurs or of its workforce.

This article provides an account of, and offers justification for, differences in the production and employment figures on which these reinterpretations are based, and reinforces the conclusions prompted by the new estimates; presents, for the first time, annual regional production estimates for the period 1830–1913; charts regional differences in OMY between 1831 and 1871 and explores explanations for these trends; and underlines the significance for an interpretation of the industry's performance after 1870 of productivity measured by output per man hour rather than by measures of yearly shift productivity. Together, this amounts to a revision in the history of trends in production, employment, productivity and performance of the British coal industry between 1830 and 1913.

Production

Pollard assumed that the appearance of the *Mineral Statistics* in 1854 marked the beginnings of a reliable and continuous contemporary source, consequently his research was directed towards the construction of estimates for the pre-statistical period, a process achieved by painstakingly assembling data from the several coalmining regions before aggregating to produce national figures. These estimates to 1850 were incorporated in Mitchell's 1984 study, which took Robert Hunt's figures from the *Mineral Statistics* from 1856 as the basis for extending the series further. Mitchell's regional breakdown of coal output, like that of Pollard, was in the form of quinquennial averages.[12]

New national and regional series were published in 1986[13] which differed from earlier estimates of output and employment for the period 1830 to 1913. Following Pollard's precedent, regional figures were presented only in the form of quinquennial averages and as percentages of national output. As these output estimates have been accepted by such a respected critic as B.R. Mitchell to be more accurate than any other series,[14] and as other historians of the industry have expressed interest in a detailed annual and regional breakdown to facilitate further research, the new estimates are presented in full for the first time in the Appendix to this article.

The major explanation for the discrepancy between Pollard's estimates (also used by Mitchell) and the new estimates is Pollard's reliance on the accuracy of Hunt's annual *Mineral Statistics*, first appearing in 1854, which supplied both a semi-official, apparently authoritative, fixed point from which Pollard could project backwards as a check on his estimates for preceding years;[15] the *Mineral Statistics* also underpinned Mitchell's output figures for the late 1850s and 1860s. However, Hunt's early figures contained serious omissions affecting both the national and county totals, which since that time have been overlooked. Some of these errors Hunt himself reported in the introduction to subsequent volumes of *Mineral Statistics*, where he also corrected previous inaccuracies; these revisions historians have hitherto ignored. In addition to Hunt's corrected *Mineral Statistics* a variety of sources and methods have been used in compiling the new series,[16] which when compared with existing estimates reveal appreciable differences, especially for certain regions.

The criticism that coal raised and burnt as waste should be excluded from production estimates, particularly because this practice was unusual outside the North-east and declined rapidly after 1870, can be rebutted with confidence.[17] The justification for including waste, which in the new estimates accounts for 13 per cent of production in 1830,[18] was that some of the unsold coal was used for road making and wagonway ballast; moreover, much of the waste in the North-east during the early nineteenth century was of a kind which when small coal prices rose later did find buyers. Equally relevant is the contemporary practice of colliery managers who typically measured all coal, including waste raised, and recorded the total in colliery accounts. For purposes of comparisons over time it seems appropriate to include waste (as did Pollard) which in any case for the purpose of exclusion is extremely difficult to estimate for regions other than in the North-east.[19] The category of coal consumed by other manufacturing industries is more problematical. The 1874–77 figures are residuals obtained by subtracting iron industry consumption plus shipments from the official production figures under the 1872 Coal Mines Regulation Act, which from 1874 have been accepted as accurate.[20] The estimates for preceding years are derived from backward extrapolations but modified in accordance with what is known about movements in population and economic development in the region, adding bunker coal to the totals where appropriate.

A minor difference is the figure for Lancashire and Cheshire in the 1850s, for Mitchell's figure of only 9.7 million tons for 1856 compares with 11.2 million tons in the Appendix. The revised figures result from a comparison of Hunt's figures with the considerably higher levels of output reported by Richard Meade in evidence to the Dearness and Scarcity Committee in 1873.[21] The figures in the Appendix were arrived at by reference to the movement of economic indicators, particularly cotton imports, as a proxy for fluctuations in manufacturing output and general levels of economic activity within the county.[22] Mitchell's output figures for the West Midlands between 1830 and 1867 are considerably lower than the new estimates yet cannot be explained by a difference in regional definition.[23] Hunt's figures, which he revised later after discovering his own misinterpretation of the weight of a 'Staffordshire boatload',[24] again ran at lower levels than those of Meade's 1873 figures. Supplementary evidence used to produce new estimates, working back from coal consumption, particularly by the iron industry, also helps to explain why the continuing importance of this region as a coal producer has been understated.[25] A similarly large discrepancy emerges from the two series for South Wales before 1873, partly because Hunt's figures underestimated lease weight by up to 20 per cent, and partly because prior to 1864 Hunt's figures refer to sales rather than to output, excluding colliery consumption and waste. The new estimates were calculated by applying a multiplier to pig iron production in the region (as in other iron producing regions);[26] by adding coal shipments,[27] and estimated coal consumed in other industries, principally copper and tinplate,[28] and, as for all other regions, including miners' coal allowances,[29] coal burnt for domestic purposes,[30] and coal used for colliery consumption and waste.

TABLE 1

ESTIMATES OF PRODUCTION IN THE MAJOR BRITISH COALFIELDS, 1831–1911
(ANNUAL PERCENTAGE GROWTH RATES, DECENNIAL AVERAGES).

	Great Britain	Scot- land	North- east	Lancs & Cheshire	York- shire	East Midlands	West Midlands	South Wales
1831–41	3.5	3.8	3.6	3.4	3.8	3.1	2.8	4.3
1841–51	4.1	5.7	3.9	4.8	4.3	3.7	3.4	3.7
1851–61	3.2	4.1	2.8	3.7	4.1	6.1	1.0	3.5
1861–71	3.1	2.9	4.5	1.5	3.4	3.8	4.6	1.8
1871–81	2.5	3.2	2.1	2.9	3.8	5.5	0.0	3.4
1881–91	1.9	2.1	1.0	2.0	2.2	3.3	0.1	3.1
1891–1901	1.9	3.2	1.8	1.7	3.2	3.5	0.0	4.0
1901–11	2.2	2.5	2.2	-0.0	3.8	2.4	1.5	2.6

Sources: Appendix 1.

The new estimates for South Wales are especially important, since they indicate that even in the 1830s output in the region was already outstripping that of Scotland, and of Lancashire and Cheshire, hitherto the third and fourth largest producers after the North-east and West Midlands. The estimates also reveal that South Wales achieved second ranking in the 1850s, followed by the West Midlands and Lancashire. The stable share of national production held by the North-east is one of the striking secular trends to emerge from the regional estimates, that region finally losing first place to South Wales in 1913. The relative importance of the West Midlands at the beginning of the period is confirmed, though at substantially higher levels than those recorded hitherto by Pollard and Mitchell. The revised estimates point to the success of Midland producers in maintaining their lead over Lancashire and Cheshire until the 1870s, when the decline of the West Midlands, falling to the bottom of the major producing regions by 1890, was rapid. By that time output from Yorkshire and the East Midlands exceeded production in the West Midlands and that from Lancashire and Cheshire. Scotland, meanwhile, after a long period of stability, increased its share of total production, sharing with South Wales in the secular expansion of coal exports beginning in the 1880s.

The differentials in growth rates (Table 1) which result from the new estimates (and are offered with confidence from the 1840s) differ from those described by Mitchell.[31] Decennial growth rates reveal a decline in the national average beginning in the 1850s, though regional rates of growth differ markedly. Throughout the period 1831–1911 the York-shire region grew at rates in excess of the national average, as did the

East Midlands from the 1850s and South Wales and the North-east from the 1870s. Scotland, too, recorded above average increases except in the 1850s and 1860s, a 5.7 per cent growth in the 1840s setting an all time record for all regions. By contrast the West Midlands recorded below average growth rates throughout the period, excepting the 1860s.[32] Lancashire experienced fluctuations and a sustained deceleration from the 1880s.

The new national output estimates require some qualification to Mitchell's conclusion that by the criterion of annual growth rates the early 1870s marked a break in trend.[33] The revised estimates reveal the point of inflection to have occurred during the cycle 1854–66, when annual compounded rates fell below three per cent for the first time over each cycle since 1815–30, the fastest rate coinciding with the cycle 1847–54.[34] The 1860s did not, therefore, witness a return to the high growth rates of the second quarter of the century as Mitchell maintains, but possibly to the lower level of 1815–30. The 1860s ushered in a period of relatively stable rates of growth, interrupted only by a temporary setback in 1883–90. Whereas historians in the past have stressed a declining growth rate from the 1870s, though especially from the late 1880s, the new output estimates reveal a broadly constant rate of expansion over the period 1874–1913 at slightly below two per cent,[35] the relatively high labour productivity of the 1880s appearing as an exceptional interlude in the industry's long-term record. These revisions prompt a re-examination of the notion that coal was in decline in late Victorian Britain.

Employment

Even if the 1986 production figures are accepted as representing a more accurate record of the industry's growth, question marks none the less surround employment and productivity, which are central to historians' interpretations of the performance and role of the coal industry in the economy before 1914. Although broadly he accepts the reliability of the new output estimates, Mitchell has questioned the validity of the new estimates of employment,[36] and by so doing casts doubt both on the productivity trends and the assessment of industrial performance described in our alternative interpretation of the industry's development. A more detailed justification for the new employment estimates, therefore, is necessary in order to defend the new interpretation.

The deficiencies of the censuses as a source of accurate information on employment are well known, and attempts have been made to adjust for their defects. Mitchell related the number of miners to the population of those districts which were the principal coal-mining areas of the country in 1841. Adjustment of the ratio to take account of the changing industrial structure of the areas was a method which he acknowledged depended on subjective judgement, both as to what constituted the 'mainly coalmining areas' at each census, and as to whether there was a clear-cut case for altering the 1841 ratio of miners to population; the figures which resulted for the census years between 1801 and 1871 he described as no more than 'informed guesses'.[37] *Victorian Pre-eminence* contained a table similarly showing national and regional estimates of coalmining employment in census years beginning in 1831, but has been described by Mitchell as 'of uncertain provenance', less robust than those presented in his own study.[38] Because of the implications of these employment estimates for con-clusions relating to productivity it is necessary to persuade historians that one or other series on offer is the more reliable, for like the output estimates before 1872 there are substantial differences and the implica-tions for productivity trends are important.

Annual figures for the period 1871–1913 have been presented elsewhere; Table 2 extends the summary table for 1830–70 from the same source to show the annual series for that period.

TABLE 2

ESTIMATES OF ANNUAL COALMINING EMPLOYMENT IN BRITAIN, 1830–70

1830	104,830	1840	149,566	1850	211,811	1860	288,052
1831	109,300	1841	153,340	1851	218,280	1861	295,810
1832	113,744	1842	160,459	1852	225,988	1862	304,879
1833	118,248	1843	166,878	1853	233,746	1863	313,948
1834	122,722	1844	173,297	1854	241,504	1864	323,017
1835	127,196	1845	179,716	1855	249,262	1865	332,086
1836	131,670	1846	186,135	1856	257,020	1866	341,155
1837	136,144	1847	192,554	1857	264,778	1867	350,224
1838	140,618	1848	198,973	1858	272,536	1868	359,293
1839	145,092	1849	205,392	1859	280,294	1869	368,362
						1870	377,431

Sources: See text and R. Church, *The History of the British Coal Industry. Volume 3: 1830–1913: Victorian Pre-eminence* (Oxford, 1986), Appendix 3.1.The figure for 1841 corrects a transposition error.

The explanation for these differences is to be found in differing methodologies in using the censuses and in supplementary evidence. The new estimates differ from those of Mitchell in the following respects: miners over the age of 65 were included, as were those in the category 'owners, agents, etc.'; another difference lies in the treatment of the 'unspecified miners' category.[39] It seemed improbable that all were coalminers, consequently the totals were divided proportionately according to the ratio of recorded coalminers to recorded metal and other miners in each county for the years 1841, 1861 and 1871, when this problem occurs.[40] Much more important than these differences, however, are the adjustments to the census figures in the light of additional contemporary evidence, notably for 1841 from the Children's Employment Commission, and later from the Mines Inspectors' Reports. Any supposition that the new employment estimates are vitiated by cross correlation between series is unjustified, though clearly in the iterative process of choosing between conflicting data a degree of consistency with movements in output was one factor taken into consideration when judging the plausibility of annual estimates figures for the 1830s. This also applies to the Inspectors' Returns employed as the basis for employment figures from 1864 onwards, though thereafter differences between Mitchell and the new estimates are relatively small and diminishing.

A defence of the straight-line backward extrapolation from 1841 to 1830 is made on the basis of information on employment in the North-east – then producing 23 per cent of national output – which was consistent with the figure which resulted. Those contemporary sources were John Buddle's evidence to the Lords Select Committee in 1829 and the M.S. Book of Collieries in the Vend, a coalowners' survey carried out in 1828. Even after making some allowance for employment in the numerous, though small, landsale collieries, a figure of 21,100 tons seemed to be a reasonably accurate estimate.[41] The assumption, prompted by the figures for the North-east which have been extended to estimate employment in other regions, should be considered within a context of an absence of evidence for more than minimal improvements in productivity outside the North-east, thereby justifying the more reliable estimates of output in that region as an acceptable (though possibly optimistic) basis for estimating trends elsewhere.

A detailed exposition of each regional estimate would be tedious, but the major differences between the new estimates[42] and the 1841 census figures (which are particularly important as they provide the basis for a straight line projection backwards to 1830) warrant further explanation. These are presented (and accompanied by Mitchell's 1841 estimates)[43] in Table 3, indicating the differences. The estimates for the North-east were increased to take account of the detailed information contained in contemporary surveys listing colliery by colliery employment. A far from complete survey, conducted in 1841–42 for the Midland Mining Commission by John Liefchild, recorded 12,833 men in 41 collieries on the Tyne, in addition to 12,937 men in 27 collieries on the Wear and Tees, a total of 25,770.[44] Additional evidence[45] made it possible to judge a figure of 31,000 for 1841 to be a defensible estimate. The Scottish estimates were adjusted to take into account the abundant information contained in the Children's Employment Commission reports for eastern Scotland, including details of male and female employment;[46] after adjustments to the census figures on the basic formula applied in constructing the new estimates, comparison with the Commission's figures required an additional 880 males and 2,253

TABLE 3

COALMINING EMPLOYMENT ESTIMATES 1841

	Mitchell estimates	New estimates	Net difference between census and recalculated census figures	Net difference between new estimates & census figures after making further adjustments
Scotland	17,500	21,110	+ 858	+4359
North-east	24,600	31,000	+ 76	+6870
Cumberland	2,100	2,500	- 3	+ 504
Lancashire & Cheshire	18,700	20,450	+ 830	+2602
North Wales	4,800	3,600	+ 32	-1027
Yorkshire	12,300	13,110	+ 66	+ 816
East Midlands	7,600	6,840	(- 914)*	(- 542)*
West Midlands	23,500	23,380	(+1123)*	(+1872)*
South Wales	25,800	24,750	+ 502	+2703
South West	7,600	6,600	+ 90	+ 113

* Mitchell's East Midlands includes Warwickshire, which in the new estimates is included with the West Midlands.

Sources: See text; B.R. Mitchell, *Economic Development of the British Coal Industry, 1800–1914* (Cambridge, 1984); Church, *Victorian Pre-eminence*, Appendix 3.1

females. This suggested that upward revisions were also justified for the west of Scotland. In the case of Lancashire and Cheshire, as for Scotland, the addition of 1,750 female mineworkers was necessary, based on evidence to the Commission, 750 in the case of Yorkshire, 750 for the East Midlands, and 650 for South Wales,[47] though the Commission and other contemporary sources suggested that a further modest upward revision to the principality's figure was justified.[48] The difference for North Wales, small in absolute terms but a relatively large discrepancy, is explained by an adjustment for lead miners on the assumption that all in the 'unspecified miner' category, and some of the 'coal miners', must have been non-coal miners, with an addition of 50 female coal miners.

The differences between Mitchell's employment figures for 1871 and the new estimates are explained by the basis of the calculations. Mitchell's figures rely on his census-based formula, whereas the new estimates used information from the Mines Inspectors' Reports, which from the mid-1870s may be regarded as very reliable. These mid-1870s figures were adjusted backwards from the trend in employment after 1873 and checked against output, recognising that the history of productivity in the industry in the period after the mid-1870s does not, except in years of widespread major industry stoppages, reveal annual variations in output per man year of more than a few percentage points. The main defect of the 1871 Census is the exclusion of females, which affects the figures for Scotland, Lancashire and Cheshire, West Midlands, South Wales and, Cumberland. On other counts the census figures were adjusted upwards for Northumberland, increasing the North-east total, for Yorkshire, East and West Midlands, South Wales and the South-west. Figures for Scotland given by the census seem to include non-coal miners, which justified reducing the number of male coal miners.[49] New estimates for employment by region between 1871 and 1913 are presented in Table 3.1 of *Victorian Pre-eminence*.

Labour Productivity

New estimates of productivity measured by OMY before 1872 are straight-line projections for employment between census years combined with production estimates (Table 4), which when compared with other series available for certain years reveal important differences (Table 5).

Mitchell's estimates imply productivity improvement by perhaps 15 per cent between the beginning and end of the 1830s, a modest fall in the 1840s, followed by a massive rise in productivity by more than one third. The 1860s are seen as years of modest productivity increase.[50] Disregarding what may have been an exceptionally high figure for 1830

TABLE 4

ESTIMATED OUTPUT PER MAN YEAR IN
THE BRITISH COAL INDUSTRY, 1831–71

1831	285	1841	285	1851	299	1861	301
1832	281	1842	275	1852	302	1862	298
1833	277	1843	275	1853	307	1863	305
1834	275	1844	276	1854	310	1864	306
1835	274	1845	283	1855	306	1865	308
1836	276	1846	285	1856	307	1866	307
1837	277	1847	280	1857	309	1867	304
1838	279	1848	284	1858	294	1868	301
1839	281	1849	288	1859	295	1869	301
1840	284	1850	295	1860	305	1870	306
						1871	314

Sources: See text.

TABLE 5

ESTIMATED OUTPUT PER MAN-YEAR IN
THE BRITISH COAL INDUSTRY, 1830–71 (IN TONS)

	Taylor	Mitchell	New Estimates
1830		215	290
1840		238	284
1845			283
1850	220	231	295
1855			306
1861	272	302	301
1866		317	307
1871	300	317	314

Sources: A.J. Taylor, 'Labour Productivity and Technological Innovation in the
British Coal Industry, 1850–1914', *Economic History Review* (1961–62),
pp.49; Mitchell, *British Coal Industry*, Table 10.1.

the new estimates in Table 5 suggest that the overall trend over the four
decades was stable and that the substantial rise in productivity in the
1850s did not occur.

Mitchell asserts that a 'respectable rate of progress' during the 1830s
followed by a decade of 'slow improvement' presents a more plausible
picture of the development of productivity than that set out in *Victorian
Pre-eminence*.[51] The flimsy basis of output and especially employment
estimates for the 1830s – as with those for Mitchell's estimates – rule out
confident assertions regarding productivity. None the less it is not easy
to accept Mitchell's account of the industry in this period. Transport
improvements and an increased use of coal in industry which resulted in
greater regularity of work in the inland coalfields are adduced in
explanation, though the increase in productivity shown in Mitchell's
table occurred principally in the coastal coalfields of the North-east and
South Wales, as well as in Lancashire and Cheshire.[52]

Supposing Mitchell's employment figures to be acceptable as
reliable estimates and combined with the new output estimates to
1871,[53] the effect is to render productivity growth dependent upon the
North-east and Scotland, and on the inland coalfields of Lancashire
and Cheshire and Yorkshire. It is true that the development of inland
coal resources in the coastal regions benefited from improvements in
river, canal and rail transport, as did the mining regions situated
entirely inland, but there is little evidence of a marked and sustained

increase in the regularity of mineworking in any of the coalfields before the 1860s, and certainly no evidence of other than a gradual movement towards more full-time employment as the market for coal expanded.[54] The new output and employment estimates imply a rate of expansion which was no more than marginally greater in the 1840s and 1850s than in the 1830s, whereas Mitchell's formula shows rising productivity in the 1830s and a drop in the 1840s.[55] When Mitchell's employment figures are combined with the new output estimates higher levels of productivity are implied for 1840 compared with 1830, followed by a fall between 1840 and 1850.

Is it plausible to regard the 1830s as a decade when productivity rose considerably more than in the 1840s? There is general agreement that mining methods, specifically the substitution of pillar and stall working by long wall mining or its variants, had a limited effect on productivity before the mid-century. The safety lamp contributed to safer coal getting in the North-east from the 1830s but in other regions adoption was slow.[56] Mitchell has argued that the use of gunpowder, substituted for pick and wedge to bring coal down, was rapidly adopted from the 1830s with 'quite a marked effect on productivity', accepting a contemporary's estimate of a rise in the output of hard coal by between 20 and 30 per cent.[57] However, the rapidity with which this innovation was diffused beyond the collieries of the North-east is open to question and in any case represented a potential gain in overall (rather than merely hewers') productivity of not more than between five and eight per cent.[58]

It is now generally agreed that most important of all factors affecting productivity were innovations in transporting coal, yet again there is little evidence to suggest that these were sufficiently dramatic or widespread to explain an appreciable rise in productivity in the 1830s. One of the key factors explaining the diffusion of advanced haulage and winding methods, after all, was the 1842 Mines Act, which forbade women and young children to work underground; it was after this legislation that ponies transformed face haulage, first in the North-east, before spreading to other coalfields.[59] In main roads horses were introduced to effect extended truck and wagon movements. Wheeled wagons, iron rails, and the use of steam power for winding on dip slopes were already widespread by 1842, and undoubtedly affected productivity in the 1830s. In the 1840s, however, steam began to be applied to main road haulage, a development facilitated by the introduction of the wire rope. By 1860 stationary steam engines in conjunction with wire ropes had largely superseded horses at the faces of many of the largest collieries in the North-east. Winding the coal from pit bottom to surface had been effected with the use of steam before 1830, but not until the 1840s were powerful engines of up to 200 horsepower introduced to exploit the strength of the new wire ropes, mainly in the North-east and Lancashire.[60] It is hardly conceivable that even in the pioneering North-eastern region those developments would have led to a substantial productivity spurt in the 1830s, and there is certainly no reason to suppose that this was common throughout other regions.

In so far as technology and mining methods were the major determinants of productivity levels in the nineteenth century, the revised productivity estimates seem to be consistent with the extent and pace of innovation, the effects of legislation, and the rate of output expansion in the coalfields, which underpin the fundamental difference in interpretation of productivity trends in the industry during the early and mid-Victorian boom.

Unmistakeably upward trends in labour productivity between 1840 and 1870 were limited to the North-east, where the level of productivity was the highest and rising, Scotland, where relatively low productivity until the mid-1840s was second only to the North-east by the late 1860s, and in the South-west. Table 6 also shows the relatively low productivity of the coalfields of Lancashire, Cheshire and North Wales and of South Wales and the South-west in the 1830s and 1840s, and the high, though declining, productivity from the 1840s to 1871 of Yorkshire (principally West Yorkshire), the East Midlands and the West Midlands (though rising in the 1860s). The other unmistakable trend is towards a convergence of productivity levels on the coalfields during the early and mid-Victorian years.

TABLE 6

REGIONAL COAL OUTPUT PER MAN YEAR, 1831–71

	1831	1841	1851	1861	1871
Scotland	214	213	246	306	323
North-east	327	323	376	382	397
Cumberland	316	320	245	281	280
Lancashire and Cheshire	279	279	280	281	272
North Wales	231	194	268	291	278
Yorkshire	319	320	298	286	291
East Midlands	333	336	307	291	288
West Midlands	315	321	299	249	326
South Wales	277	283	310	326	291
South West	151	152	176	174	183

Sources: See text. Calculations of annual output per man year for the period were made by combining output estimates with employment figures derived by fitting a linear time trend to decennial values. The trends described in the text are supported by those estimates.

Explanations of these findings are not easy to find in the absence of detailed regional histories, though speculation on the basis of published research is certainly possible in respect of some of the major coalmining regions. The striking improvement in productivity in the North-east and a sustained superiority compared with other regions is the easiest to explain, for this region is widely acknowledged to have been in the vanguard with respect to the introduction of innovation in ventilation and other safety measures, shot firing, haulage, and winding, besides which the continuity of production made possible by the distributive arrangements for the export of coal to London which underpinned a relatively reliable overseas market, was another important factor. The extremely low productivity of the Scottish coalfields is more difficult to explain, except perhaps in geological terms, but the rise in OMY in the 1850s and 1860s has been explained by Youngson Brown mainly by the shift from pillar and stall to long wall methods of mining, reinforced, partly as cause and partly as effect, of the high level of output consequent on the development of the blackband seams, which by generating high output – and therefore employment levels – raised productivity.[61] East Scotland was also the coalfield most affected by the legislation affecting women workers underground, which sharpened the spur towards transport innovation.[62] The declining productivity of Lancashire and Cheshire is probably explicable in terms of geology, as is the decline in Yorkshire, where the highly productive seams of South Yorkshire had yet to yield their potential, and as are the productivity trends in South Wales.

Hitherto historians have focused on productivity trends after 1870 and explanation for the decline, identified as a well-established trend. Estimates recalculated by Mitchell generally confirm this picture of declining OMY and OMS, the origins of which he locates in the 1880s.

The productivity movements described by Mitchell after 1870 derived from the division of output by the statutory employment returns to the Mines Inspectors under the Coal Mines Regulation Act of 1872.[63] This is misleading, however, for the Act applied also to workers in stratified ironstone, shale and fireclay mines, who after 1894 were excluded from the official statistics.[64] In the mid-1870s, by which time the Act was working smoothly,[65] roughly eight per cent of the recorded numbers may be estimated to have been employed outside coal mines, falling to six per cent in 1885 and two per cent by 1913.[66] The effects of these changing levels of under-recording, unless sub-contracted from the total, is to distort calculations of productivity, especially for the shale and ironstone-producing region of Scotland, and for the West Midlands which includes the North Staffordshire ironstone workers. None the less, the unmistakable trend in OMY from the late 1880s, and in OMS beginning in the mid 1880s, was that of decline.[67]

Historians have set this decline within a context of diminishing returns, the ageing of collieries, and the dominance of excessive numbers of collieries too small to benefit from economies of scale. Evidence for all or any of these factors is offered as justification either for allegations of entrepreneurial weakness, or at best an entrepreneurial rationality constrained by geology, relative factor prices, and the market; which taken together warrant exoneration for failing to achieve OMY levels which were to be found in American and German coalfields.

Analysis of coalfield and colliery records has cast doubt on the statistical basis defining the problem, and therefore raises questions about the validity of the explanations advanced.[68] Econometric exercises which tested data for South Wales, Monmouthshire and the North-east found neither inverse relationships between colliery productivity levels and age, nor convincing evidence for the existence of economies of scale.[69] Boyns's detailed statistical analysis of changes in labour productivity over cycles between 1889 and 1913 revealed that neither the boom of 1895–1900 nor of 1904–7 led to major falls in OMY, allegedly due to diminishing returns. This prompted him to question the validity of the received notion that diminishing returns were undermining the industry's performance. Boyns concluded that much more important influences on the industry's record, measured by the criteria of OMY or OMS, both in the short and in the longer term between 1890 and 1913, were the state of trade, the number of days worked, and the duration of shifts.[70] Boyns has not been alone in noticing the relevance to productivity of hours worked, which has also engaged the attention of Phelps Brown, and later Hirsch and Hausmann, each of whom placed hours reduction as part of their explanation for productivity decline in the industry.[71] This line of argument is consistent with the view that after the Coal Mines Regulation Act of 1872, which limited young persons' work underground and indirectly restricted the working hours of adult miners, neither OMY nor OMS offer adequate measures of efficiency; for this reason it is argued that while before 1872 OMY offers a helpful guide to movements in labour productivity, after 1872 the appropriate measure of labour productivity is output per man hour.[72]

For the pre-1872 period, when hours reduction was limited, OMY figures may be accepted as a more reliable guide to efficiency in the industry – at least between the Mines Acts of 1842 and 1872. In combination the new estimates of output and employment present a less dramatic course of labour productivity than that portrayed in the literature, which hitherto has dominated interpretations of the industry and its role in the economy. The revised national picture is that of a slow, barely perceptible rise to a decade of relatively stable productivity in the 1860s. This was followed by a discontinuity in the form of a sharp fluctuation during the great boom of the early 1870s. The rise in OMY/OMS to a peak in 1883 did not, therefore, represent a continuation of an upward secular trend interrupted by the boom, but an exceptional, relatively shortlived rise in productivity which coincided with the cycle.[73]

Estimates of output per man-hour also indicate a reversal of a temporary upward movement in productivity in the 1880s, followed by a recovery to relatively stable levels of hourly productivity. The fall began after the implementation of the Eight Hours Act of 1908.[74] Hirsch and Hausmann have adduced hours reduction as a major factor in explaining a decline in OMY, which we would endorse.[75] However, estimates of hourly productivity, which reflect more accurately the relationship between labour input and coal production, suggest that contrary to the accepted view based on estimates of OMY and OMS, levels of productivity in the 1900s actually exceeded those of the mid-nineteenth century.[76] From which it may be deduced that the secular deterioration in productivity between 1880 and 1914, hitherto regarded as central to the industry's history, is at least an exaggeration – and is probably a myth.

University of East Anglia, Norwich

NOTES

I am indebted to Alan Hall and John Kanefsky for their assistance in the assembly of data for the series of estimates which form the basis of this article, and to an anonymous referee for constructive advice on statistical presentation.

1. N.F.R. Crafts, *British Economic Growth during the Industrial Revolution* (Oxford, 1985), especially pp.146–7; Rondo Cameron, 'A New View of European Industrialization', *Economic History Review*, Vol. XXXVIII, No.1 (1985), pp.1–23.
2. Sidney Pollard, 'A New Estimate of British Coal Production, 1750–1850', *Economic History Review*, Vol. XXXIII, No.2 (1980), pp.212–32.
3. Coal was also an industry possessing a high value added yield. An 1871 survey recorded materials and stores at 12 per cent of colliery working costs (Roy Church, with the assistance of Alan Hall and John Kanefsky, *The History of the British Coal Industry. Volume 3: 1830–1913: Victorian Pre-eminence* (Oxford, 1986), p.505, which compares with figures for 'materials and services' of 12 per cent in the 1907 *Census of Production*. Taking into account the increase in mechanisation between 1831 and 1907 a figure of ten per cent is a reasonable guess. On this assumption, and using the new output estimates referred to below, value added in the coal industry is caluctated at £9.9m, 25 per cent greater than that shown in Crafts' comparisons of value added in British industry for 1831, Table 2.3.
4. Pollard, art. cit., p.212.
5. Ibid., B.R. Mitchell, *Economic Development of the British Coal Industry, 1800–1914* (Cambridge, 1984), Ch.3, especially pp.40–53. Charles H. Feinstein and Sidney Pollard, *Studies in Capital Formation in the United Kingdom, 1750–1920* (Oxford, 1988) pp.35–72, 281–6.
6. B.R. Mitchell, op. cit., Table 1.1, p.3.
7. Ibid., pp.325, 328.
8. J.H. Clapham, referred to the 'product of labour' after 1871 which continued to increase 'but slower for another decade; then retrogression set in'. *An Economic History of Modern Britain Vol. III; Free Trade and Steel* (Cambridge, 1932, pp.103–4; A.J. Taylor, 'Labour Productivity and Technological Innovation in the British

Coal Industry, 1850–1914', *Economic History Review*, Second Series (1961–62) pp.48–70; 'The Coal Industry', in D.H. Aldcroft (ed.), *The Development of British Industry and Foreign Competition, 1875–1914* (London, 1968), pp.37–70. See also discussions in the textbooks by Francois Crouzet, *The Victorian Economy* (1980), pp.268–71, and Peter Mathias, *The First Industrial Nation* (1981), pp.377–8, and R.C. Floud and D.N. McCloskey, *The Economic History of Britain since 1700*, Vol. II (1981), pp.116–18.

9. Matthews, Feinstein and Odling Smee, op. cit., pp.229, 232–3, 462–7.
10. See Barry T. Hirsch and William J. Hausmann, 'Labour Productivity in the British and South Wales Coal Industry, 1874–1914', *Economica*, N.S. 50 (1983), pp.145–57; David Greasley, 'Wage Rates and Work Intensity in the South Wales Coalfield, 1874–1914', *Economica*, N.S. 52 (1985), pp.383–9; Peter Wardley, 'Labouring and Productivity Estimates: A Comment on Hirsch and Hausmann's Model of Coal Miners' Productivity, 1874–1914', *Economica*, N.S. 54 (1987), pp.521–4; Barry T. Hirsch and William J. Hausmann, 'Labouring: A Reply', *Economica*, N.S. 54 (1987), p.525.
11. B.R. Mitchell has commented on some of the differences in his review of *The History of the British Coal Industry Volume 3: 1830–1913 Victorian Pre-eminence*, in *Business History*, Vol.XXIX, No.2 (1987), pp.222–3.
12. Mitchell, *Economic Development of the British Coal Industry*, Tables 1.1 and 1.3.
13. Church, op. cit., Table 1.1 and 1.2.
14. Mitchell, loc. cit., pp.222–3.
15. Pollard, art. cit., p.214.
16. For sources see Church, op. cit., Appendix 1.1.
17. Mitchell, loc. cit., pp.222–3. However, Mitchell adopted Pollard's pre-1850 estimates – which did *include* waste. Pollard, op. cit., pp.217–9.
18. Church, op. cit., Appendix 1.1.
19. Evidence on waste and colliery consumption in 1869 can be found for most of the coalmining districts in the *Coal Supply Commission* 1871 C.435 Committee E. In addition to the North-east sizeable amounts of waste may be attributed to Lancashire, the West Midlands, South Wales and Scotland. The total volume of colliery consumption, however, was underestimated, as Hunt's 1873 *Mineral Statistics* show (p.xvi).
20. Finlay Gibson, *A Compilation of Statistics of the Coalmining Industry* (Cardiff, 1922), preface.
21. *Report from the Select Committee on the Present Dearness and Scarcity of Coal*, 1873 (313) X, Appendix 3, pp.356–7, 1, Richard Meade's figures exceeded the estimate in Table 1, see 9911–12.
22. Information relating to steam power in the 1830s and in 1869 is to be found in the Factory Returns *Accounts and Papers*, 1836, XLV, pp.307–10 and 1839, XLI, pp.114–333; *Report of the Commissioners into Coal*, 1871 C.435, Committee E, appendices, also includes information specifically on coal consumption.
23. Warwickshire is included in the East Midlands in Mitchell's regional breakdown.
24. Samuel Bailey, 'The Economic Value ... of the South Staffordshire Coalfield', in Samuel Timmins (ed.), *Birmingham and the Midlands Hardware District* (1866 reprinted Cass, London, 1967), p.28.
25. Of particular importance in estimating coal consumed in iron production in the region was T. Smith, *The Miner's Guide* (London, 1836) p.87, also the Coal Supply Commission 1871 C.435, Committee E, J.P. Baker's reports to Chief Inspector of Mines in the 1860s and 1870s, and E.G. Grant, 'The Spatial Development of the Warwickshire Coalfield' (unpublished Ph.D. thesis, University of Birmingham, 1969) pp.245, 338.
26. Coal consumed in iron production, including all intermediate processes in the making of bars and similar items for use by manufacturing and transport industries, was six tons per ton in 1854 declining gradually to five tons by 1874, and was a major source of discrepancy. Compare the estimate by Truman, formerly works manager of Dowlais, of 6.52 tons required in 1854 in South Wales where an appreciable

amount of pig iron imported from Scotland was processed into bars and rails. William Truran, *The Iron Manufacture of Great Britain* (London, 1855), pp.168–9, 175–6. In 1873 the Dearness and Scarcity Commission, put coal consumed at three tons per ton of pig, plus three tons seven cwts for converting into malleable iron, castings, etc. Other evidence from the same source refers to 2.5 tons as the ratio for processing in South Wales in 1872. As this agrees with later data, a figure of 2.5 ton for pig iron production and a further 2.5 for conversion seemed to be justified, though perhaps conservative before 1860. *Report from the Select Committee on the Present Dearness and Scarcity of Coal*, 1873 (313) X, 1, pp.34–5, 347.

27. Coal shipments present only a minor problem in that the official figures of coal shipped coastwise or exported include coke and patent fuel and are therefore not convertible into coal equivalent. The actual amounts involved are likely to have been small and the understatement of coal consumed in coke production is to some extent offset by the 90 per cent ratio of coal to patent fuel production. After 1873 the figures were officially adjusted on the basis that ten tons of coal made six of coke and nine tons made ten tons of patent fuel.

28. Other key sources were M. Dunn, *A Treatise on the Winning and Working of Collieries* (Newcastle, 1852), p.51, and the *Coal Supply Commission* 1871, C.435 Committee E.

29. Regional estimates from Alexander Smith, 'The Allowance Coal Question' (Dudley Herald Office, 1875), pp.1–16; *Samuel Commission*, Vol.III, Appendix 18.

30. The assumption that domestic consumption was one ton per capita was based on evidence from Prospectus, Report of the Darlington and Stockton Railway, 1821. *Report of the Select Committee of the House of Lords on the State of the Coal Trade 1830* (9) viii, 405, p.71.

31. Mitchell, op. cit., pp.7–8.

32. Warwickshire is included in West Midlands.

33. Mitchell, op. cit., p.3.

34. Church, op. cit., Table 1.1 and Table 2 (above).

35. Corroboration of this conclusion, applying multiple regression analysis, is provided by T. Boyns, 'Labour Productivity in the British Coal Industry, 1874–1913' (unpublished Ph.D. thesis, University of Wales, 1982), p.33.

36. Mitchell, loc. cit.

37. Mitchell, op. cit.

38. Mitchell, loc. cit.

39. There is evidence that miners aged 65, or over did not necessarily leave the industry, but took less onerous jobs. Church, op. cit., p.300. Mitchell included all unspecified miners in 1841 and 1861, though not in 1871.

40. The formula was $[C = U \dfrac{c}{c-m}]$. Some differences occur as a result of our respective interpretations of whether female workers in non-coal mining counties were coalminers (in 1841 the new estimates include only those in coalmining counties); or to whom 'female labourers' referred (in 1861 the new estimates exclude these). Mitchell's figure for females in 1871 is comprised principally of metal miners, mostly in Cornwall.

41. North of England Institute of Mining and Mechanical Engineers, Newcastle, Buddle Atkinson Collection, Shelf 45, Vol.5 (unpaginated); *Report of the Select Committee of the House of Lords on the State of the Coal Trade 1830* (9) viii, 405, p.54; see also North of England Institute, Miscellaneous Deposits, ZC/14–15, Coalowners' Returns, 1843.

42. Church, op. cit., Table 3.1.

43. Mitchell, op. cit., Table 5.3.

44. *Report of the Commissioners on the Condition of the Mining Population of South Staffordshire Coalfield*, 1843 (508) XIII.1, pp.107–8.

45. *Reports of the Commissioners ... on the Mining Districts*, 1847 (844) XVI, pp.31–2, 423, and the 1844 list originally published in the *Newcastle Journal* and reproduced

in the *Second Report of the Select Committee on Accidents in Coal Mines*, 1854 (169) IX, pp.93–4.

46. *Children's Employment Commission* 1842, XVI, Appendix 1, pp.387–9.
47. *Children's Employment Commission* 1842 (38) XV, pp.36–43, 50–51.
48. *Children's Employment Commission* 1842 (381) XVI, R.H. Franks Report pp.387–9.
49. For more detailed explanation see Church, op. cit., Appendix 3.1.
50. Mitchell, op. cit., Table 10.1; Church, op. cit., Table 6.1.
51. Mitchell, loc. cit.
52. Mitchell, op. cit., Table 10.1
53. This is an alternative formula suggested by Mitchell, review cited.
54. Church, op. cit., pp.6, 38–40, 248–9, 547.
55. Mitchell, review cited.
56. Church, op. cit., p.327.
57. Mitchell, op. cit., pp.75–6.
58. Church, op. cit., pp.340–42.
59. Ibid., p.365.
60. A.J. Taylor, 'The Coal Industry' in Roy Church (ed.), *The Dynamics of Victorian Business* (1980), pp.53–4; Church, *Victorian Pre-eminence*, pp.367–71.
61. A.J. Youngson Brown, 'The Scots Coal Industry, 1853–86' (unpublished thesis, University of Aberdeen, 1952–53), pp.66–74.
62. *Children's Employment Commission* 1842 (381) XVI, pp.387–9.
63. Mitchell, op. cit., pp.106–7, Table 5.4.
64. *Reports of the Mines Inspectors; Mineral Statistics.*
65. Finlay Gibson regarded the 1874 return as the first complete, and therefore reliable, set of employment figures collected under the Act. F.A. Gibson, *A Compilation of Statistics of the Coalmining Industry* (Cardiff, 1922), preface.
66. The method used to adjust figures to 1894 (when the non coal miners were separately categorized) is explained in Church, op. cit., Appendix 3.1, especially pp.301–2.
67. Church, op. cit., Fig 6.1, p.473.
68. Church, op. cit., pp.473–88.
69. Boyns, thesis, pp.211, 273, 355.
70. Ibid., pp.361–6.
71. E.II. Phelps Brown and M.H. Browne, *A Century of Pay* (1968), pp.175–82; B.T. IIirsch and W.J. Hausmann, 'Labour Productivity in the British and South Wales Coal Industry, 1870–1914', *Economica*, N.S. 50 (1983), pp.145–57.
72. For a discussion of the weaknesses of OMY as a measure of labour productivity see Church, op. cit., pp.471–5.
73. Ibid., pp.473, 488. Using his own revised estimates of coalmining output and employment from 1864 to 1913 Boyns drew a similar conclusion, Boyns, thesis, pp.33, 45, 53, 80.
74. Ibid., Ch.6, especially pp.473–80.
75. Barry T. Hirsch and William J. Hausmann, 'Labour Productivity in the British and South Wales Coal Industry, 1874–1914', *Economica*, N.S. 50 (1983), pp.145–57.
76. Church, op. cit., Table 6.2.

APPENDIX
ESTIMATES OF ANNUAL COAL OUTPUT BY REGION, 1830–1913 (MILLION TONS)

	Scotland	North east	Cumberland	Lancashire & Cheshire	North Wales	Yorkshire	East midlands	West midlands	South Wales	South-west	Total
1831	3.1	7.0	0.6	4.1	0.6	2.9	1.7	5.7	4.6	0.8	31.1
1832	3.2	7.1	0.6	4.2	0.6	3.0	1.8	5.9	4.8	0.8	32.0
1833	3.3	7.2	0.6	4.3	0.6	3.1	1.8	6.1	5.0	0.8	32.8
1834	3.4	7.4	0.6	4.4	0.6	3.2	1.8	6.3	5.2	0.8	33.7
1835	3.5	7.8	0.7	4.5	0.6	3.3	1.9	6.5	5.4	0.8	35.1
1836	3.6	8.0	0.7	4.7	0.7	3.4	1.9	6.7	5.7	0.9	36.3
1837	3.8	8.4	0.7	4.9	0.7	3.5	1.9	6.9	6.0	0.9	37.7
1838	4.0	8.8	0.7	5.1	0.7	3.6	2.0	7.1	6.3	0.9	39.2
1839	4.2	9.1	0.7	5.3	0.7	3.8	2.1	7.3	6.6	0.9	40.7
1840	4.5	9.5	0.8	5.5	0.7	4.0	2.2	7.5	6.9	0.9	42.5
1841	4.5	10.0	0.8	5.7	0.7	4.2	2.3	7.5	7.0	1.0	43.7
1842	4.5	10.0	0.8	5.9	0.7	4.3	2.4	7.5	7.0	1.0	44.1
1843	4.6	10.3	0.8	6.2	0.8	4.5	2.5	8.0	7.2	1.0	45.9
1844	5.0	10.3	0.8	6.5	0.8	4.8	2.6	8.5	7.5	1.0	47.5
1845	5.4	11.3	0.8	6.8	0.9	5.0	2.7	9.0	8.0	1.1	51.0
1846	5.8	11.4	0.8	7.1	1.0	5.2	2.8	9.3	8.5	1.1	53.0
1847	5.8	12.0	0.8	7.4	1.0	5.4	2.9	9.0	8.5	1.1	53.9
1848	6.4	12.4	0.8	7.8	1.1	5.6	3.0	9.2	9.0	1.2	56.5
1849	7.0	12.8	0.9	8.2	1.1	5.8	3.1	9.7	9.4	1.2	59.2
1850	7.4	14.0	0.9	8.6	1.2	6.1	3.2	10.0	9.7	1.3	62.4
1851	7.8	14.6	0.9	9.1	1.3	6.4	3.3	10.4	10.0	1.3	65.1
1852	8.2	15.2	0.9	9.6	1.4	6.7	3.4	10.9	10.5	1.4	68.2
1853	8.5	15.8	0.9	10.1	1.5	7.0	3.5	11.4	11.0	1.4	71.1
1854	9.0	16.6	0.9	10.8	1.6	7.3	3.7	12.0	11.6	1.5	75.0
1855	9.0	16.6	0.9	11.0	1.6	7.8	3.6	12.0	12.4	1.4	76.3
1856	9.3	16.6	0.9	11.2	1.5	9.1	3.9	12.0	12.9	1.5	78.9
1857	10.2	17.9	0.9	11.4	1.5	8.9	4.4	11.6	13.8	1.2	81.3
1858	10.2	17.9	0.9	11.5	1.6	8.3	4.7	11.0	13.0	1.1	80.2
1859	10.8	17.9	1.0	11.7	1.6	8.2	5.3	11.1	13.8	1.3	82.7
1860	11.1	19.3	1.2	12.3	1.8	9.2	5.7	11.5	14.2	1.5	87.8

cont.

	Scotland	North east	Cumber- land	Lancashire & Cheshire	North Wales	Yorkshire	East midlands	West midlands	South Wales	South- west	Total
1861	11.6	19.1	1.3	13.0	1.9	9.4	5.9	11.4	14.0	1.5	89.1
1862	12.2	19.9	1.3	11.4	1.7	9.3	6.0	13.1	14.3	1.8	91.0
1863	12.3	22.7	1.3	11.7	1.7	9.4	6.1	14.3	14.1	2.0	95.6
1864	12.7	23.7	1.4	12.4	2.0	8.8	6.2	14.9	14.9	2.0	99.0
1865	12.8	25.4	1.4	12.8	2.0	9.4	6.7	15.4	14.4	1.9	102.2
1866	13.5	25.6	1.5	13.2	2.1	9.7	7.2	14.7	15.4	1.9	104.8
1867	14.1	25.3	1.5	13.8	2.4	9.8	7.2	14.8	15.4	2.0	106.3
1868	14.7	26.5	1.4	13.7	2.4	9.8	7.1	15.1	15.4	2.0	108.1
1869	14.6	26.1	1.4	15.0	2.2	10.8	7.7	15.9	15.1	2.0	110.8
1870	14.9	27.9	1.4	14.7	2.3	10.6	7.9	17.2	16.5	2.0	115.4
1871	15.4	29.5	1.4	14.8	2.5	12.8	8.5	17.6	16.6	2.1	121.2
1872	15.4	29.2	1.2	16.6	2.6	14.6	9.9	16.6	16.9	2.0	125.0
1873	16.9	29.6	1.2	16.8	2.5	15.3	10.7	16.7	16.2	2.0	127.9
1874	16.8	30.5	1.0	16.1	2.4	14.8	11.4	15.8	16.5	1.8	127.1
1875	18.6	32.2	1.2	18.6	2.4	15.9	11.6	16.5	14.2	1.9	133.3
1876	19.7	32.3	1.4	18.0	2.4	15.1	11.4	15.9	17.0	1.8	134.1
1877	18.3	31.4	1.4	18.3	2.5	15.8	12.0	15.5	16.9	1.8	134.1
1878	17.8	30.1	1.4	18.7	2.2	15.6	12.4	15.0	17.4	1.8	132.6
1879	17.5	28.8	1.5	19.3	2.2	16.2	13.0	15.2	17.8	2.0	133.7
1880	18.3	34.9	1.7	19.8	2.4	17.5	13.4	15.7	21.2	2.0	147.0
1881	20.8	35.6	1.8	19.3	2.7	18.3	14.4	16.9	22.3	2.1	154.2
1882	20.5	36.3	1.8	20.5	2.4	18.5	14.5	17.0	22.8	2.0	156.5
1883	21.2	37.4	1.8	21.2	2.8	19.6	15.4	17.1	25.0	2.0	163.7
1884	21.2	36.1	1.7	20.8	2.6	19.2	14.8	16.5	25.6	2.2	160.8
1885	21.3	35.1	1.7	21.3	2.3	18.5	15.7	16.8	24.3	2.2	159.4
1886	20.4	34.8	1.8	21.3	2.6	19.4	15.5	15.4	24.2	2.2	157.5
1887	21.5	34.5	1.8	21.5	2.7	20.1	15.8	15.9	26.0	2.2	162.1
1888	22.3	37.7	1.7	21.8	2.7	20.6	16.6	16.8	27.4	2.2	169.9
1889	23.2	39.1	1.7	22.3	2.9	22.0	18.0	17.2	28.1	2.2	176.9
1890	24.3	39.7	1.7	22.8	3.0	22.3	18.8	17.1	29.4	2.3	181.6

cont.

	Scotland	North east	Cumber- land	Lancashire & Cheshire	North Wales	Yorkshire	East midlands	West midlands	South Wales	South- west	Total
1891	25.4	39.1	1.7	23.4	3.2	22.8	19.8	17.8	30.0	2.3	185.5
1892	27.2	33.4	1.4	23.0	3.0	23.2	19.8	17.4	31.2	2.1	181.8
1893	25.5	39.9	1.8	16.5	2.2	16.0	14.4	16.1	30.2	1.7	164.3
1894	21.5	42.1	2.1	23.9	3.2	23.4	19.8	16.8	33.4	2.1	188.3
1895	28.8	39.8	1.9	22.8	2.8	22.8	19.3	16.1	33.0	2.1	189.7
1896	28.3	41.8	1.9	23.4	2.9	23.9	19.9	17.1	33.9	2.1	195.4
1897	29.1	43.6	2.0	23.6	2.9	24.1	21.2	17.6	35.8	2.2	202.1
1898	30.2	45.3	2.1	25.0	3.2	25.6	23.1	18.1	26.7	2.6	202.0
1899	31.4	46.1	2.1	25.1	3.2	26.9	24.7	18.4	39.9	2.5	220.1
1900	33.1	46.3	2.0	125.5	3.1	28.2	26.0	18.8	39.3	2.6	225.2
1901	32.8	45.2	2.1	24.3	3.1	27.0	25.1	17.7	39.2	2.5	219.0
1902	34.2	46.4	2.2	24.9	3.2	28.0	26.3	18.2	41.3	2.5	227.1
1903	35.0	47.9	2.2	25.0	3.2	28.5	25.9	18.0	42.2	2.4	230.3
1904	35.4	48.4	2.1	24.5	3.0	28.8	26.2	17.7	43.7	2.4	232.4
1905	35.8	50.1	2.2	24.2	2.9	29.9	27.3	18.0	43.2	2.3	236.1
1906	38.0	52.1	2.2	25.2	3.2	32.5	29.3	18.8	47.1	2.5	251.1
1907	40.1	54.0	2.3	26.6	3.5	35.2	32.6	20.7	50.0	2.8	267.8
1908	39.2	53.9	2.1	24.5	3.4	34.9	30.7	19.8	50.2	2.7	261.5
1909	39.8	55.3	2.3	24.0	3.3	35.9	30.6	19.5	50.4	2.6	263.8
1910	41.3	52.6	2.2	23.8	3.4	38.3	31.2	20.2	48.7	2.7	264.4
1911	41.7	56.4	2.3	24.0	3.4	39.1	31.6	20.4	50.2	2.6	271.9
1912	39.5	51.3	2.1	23.1	3.3	38.3	30.5	19.6	50.1	2.6	260.4
1913	42.5	56.4	2.3	24.6	3.5	43.7	33.7	20.8	56.8	3.0	287.4

Sources: See text and Church, *Victorian Pre-eminence*, Appendix 1.1.

'WEALTHY AND TITLED PERSONS' – THE ACCUMULATION OF RICHES IN VICTORIAN BRITAIN: THE CASE OF PETER DENNY

NICHOLAS MORGAN AND MICHAEL MOSS

> I believe the people of this country need to have set before them examples of moderate expenditure upon self, and of larger expenditure in a happier and unselfish way. The vulgarly ostentatious scale of expenditure which is now the fashion of many wealthy and aristocratic persons is steadily debasing our ideal of life.
>
> William Denny III to Rev. Frederick H. Naylor, 11 August 1885, quoted in A.B. Bruce, *The Life of William Denny Shipbuilder* (London, 1889), p.347.

Dives captivated the Victorian mind as much as Lazarus. Although merchant princes who had risen from humble origins had been familiar figures on the social and economic landscape in the eighteenth century, never before had so many people benefited from rising prosperity. The pursuit of business fortunes captivated all. Writing in 1845 Benjamin Disraeli looked back on the years since the great Reform Act, concluding that 'to acquire, to accumulate, to plunder each other by virtue of philosophic phrases, to propose a Utopia to consist only of WEALTH and TOIL, this has been the breathless business of enfranchised England for the last twelve years'.[1] There was a fascination with those who had succeeded in commerce or industry. Popular journals and the specialist trade and technical press were filled with biographical sketches of men of business. Regional collections of biographies brought together from county and town the lives and careers of those wealthy magnates whose evident enterprise, prodigious fortunes, and philanthropic munificence provided exemplars for the less fortunate but equally ambitious to follow.[2]

John Logan, a Glasgow grocer, lectured his colleagues on 'Success in Business' in December 1897: 'The primary and important helps to success in business', he said:

> were natural ability and fitness, bent of mind, individuality and intuition of character, in short, commercial genius, instinct and readiness of mind, knowing how to take people and meet cases, soundness of judgement enabling them to measure men and women and estimate prohibitions, alertness of observation, tact

and address, organisation, the power of mastering and working out details with promptness, decision, thoroughness, and intelligence.[3]

Such platitudinous advice was typical, deriving from the ideas of Samuel Smiles, the prophet of self-help and the self-made man. A few commentators were keen to know why some businessmen succeeded and others failed. John Logan advised would-be grocers to:

> use caution and keep within their limits. It was a mistake to expand too much at first on fixtures and utensils, the sum for which might be limited to from 10 to 15 per cent of the capital. Cash payments for first orders, and thereafter as prudent and practicable should be made ... To stock a shop properly was most important and had a great bearing on success. Light stocks in proportion to trade were very essential.[4]

Such practical guidance was rarely published; most entrepreneurs were left to learn these lessons either from the experience of their fathers or for themselves.[5]

By the beginning of the nineteenth century it was already evident that there were enormous inequalities in the distribution of wealth in society. Writing in 1824 William Thompson in his *Inquiry into the Principles of the Distribution of Wealth most conducive to Human Happiness* declared 'the great and paramount moral blessing, consequent on equal security, produced by the natural laws of distribution', was 'that excessive poverty and excessive wealth being removed from society, the peculiar vices of luxury and want would almost cease'.[6] This debate about distribution gathered force as new fortunes were amassed, and was linked to attempts by statisticians (aided by batteries of quill-wielding clerks) to penetrate Income Tax returns and, after 1894, those of the new Estate Duties in order to estimate the true wealth of the nation.[7] Neither of these methods was satisfactory; widespread evasion under Schedule D, which depended 'on the conscience of the tax-payer who often, it is to be feared, returns hundreds instead of thousands, and who is certain to decide any question that he can persuade himself to think is doubtful in his own favour', resulted in a massive underestimate of the nation's national income derived from businesses.[8] The Estate Duties were similarly subject to systematic evasion, largely through the undeclared transfer of property to relatives: Sir Charles Dilke, President of the Royal Statistical Society, concluded before a meeting of that body in 1908 that:

> they all had friends who made no secret of the disposition that they or their fathers were making of property; and many of them thought that it was no wrong to the State and nothing of which any man should be ashamed, and that it caused property to pass into hands where it would be better used than by the rich old men who held it.[9]

Whatever their failings, data derived from the collection of these two taxes persuaded many that the distribution of wealth was skewed grotesquely towards the very rich. L.G. Chiozza Money argued that 'more than one third of the entire income of the United Kingdom is enjoyed by less than one-thirtieth of its people'; turning to the Estate Duties he concluded that 'in an average year, eight millionaires die leaving between them three times as much wealth as is left by 644,000 poor persons who die in one year ... the wealth left by a few rich people who die approaches in amount the aggregate property possessed by the whole of the living poor'.[10]

One solution to the many problems perceived by Chiozza Money, a Liberal who later joined the Labour Party, was the nationalisation of land.[11] Other social reformers had singled out landed and unearned income for particular criticism. F.W. Headely in his *Darwinism and Modern Socialism*, published in 1909, attacked those who lived off their investments as 'parasitic' on the workers, and inherited fortunes as clogging the wheels of enterprise. He was delighted that the Liberal government proposed to tax unearned income more heavily than earned income.[12] Not all Liberal commentators, however, agreed with such distributionist views. The Liverpool textile magnate, philanthropist and Liberal politician, Samuel Smith, censured those who advocated Land Nationalisation at the turn of the century:

> I admit with deep sorrow that modern civilization has failed to eradicate poverty and suffering among large sections of the population ... but the causes of inequality of wealth lie deep in the foundation of human nature and the constitution of the world, and no laws can essentially alter them. Mankind vary enormously in natural and acquired gifts; it is impossible to hinder a strong man succeeding where a weak man fails, or a wise man rising where a foolish man falls ... Modern civilization does not diminish but accentuate moral and intelligent differences; it is more difficult for the idle, the improvident and the vicious to hold their own in the race of life now than in ruder ages – all our processes are more refined – all require greater skill and higher character and there is an increased tendency to precipitate the coarser material to the bottom of the social edifice ... These laws are unchangeable; they have operated in all ages and all times and human legislation cannot override them, nor should it try to do so. Yet benevolence has its function as well, as much that the State cannot do ought to be done by private philanthropy.[13]

The moral duty of the rich to make charitable provision for the poor was an accepted precept of the Victorian world. What worried many social observers was the inadequacy of such voluntary efforts to provide for the needs of the poor, particularly during periods of economic depression. Cosmo Gordon Lang, the Archbishop of York and no liberal, lent his support to arguments for redistribution when private endeavour to cure economic and social ills appeared to have totally failed during industrial disputes in the early twentieth century.[14] Others were equally troubled that the responsibilities of wealth were not being observed: 'of this growing flood of wealth', wrote the economist William Smart, 'much is abused, and, if all that were to come of this conquest of nature is increasing self-indulgence, there might not be a great deal to be thankful for'.[15]

Consumption, the *use* of wealth, was of paramount importance in determining the increase and distribution of wealth: 'in the idler wealth comes to an end, in the worker it turns into muscle and brain power, and is eternally reproduced by them'.[16] For Smart, a former businessman turned economist and economic historian, the process of wealth creation was less problematic than its dissipation. For most of his contemporaries however it was in the mechanics of wealth creation that the interesting questions remained.

At a time when the majority of concerns were organised as partnerships, it was almost impossible to penetrate the privacy of financial records to discover how fortunes were amassed or their precise size and disposition. R.S. Surtees' character Mr Joseph Large, a 'rich, very rich' teapot handle manufacturer, was typical in keeping 'all his balance sheets to himself, not even showing them to his beloved Mrs. Large'.[17] The only time the wealth of businessmen like Mr Large became visible was at death when executors were required to value an estate so that duty could be assessed. Summaries of these valuations for larger estates appeared in the press where they attracted comment from both those who admired an economy that could generate such holdings and those who deplored it.[18] Not surprisingly it was the huge riches that received the most attention. Modern scholars have been equally beguiled, compiling lists from these valuations of millionaires, half millionaires and those possessed of £100,000 or more.[19] There has been little attempt by historians to follow Chiozza Money's lead and set these great estates at death in the context of overall wealth holding or to explore the economic function of their creation and management over a lifetime. To advance the historical debate into these areas is practical; but necessarily time consuming involving the collection of a mass of data.

A start has been made through the analysis of detailed inventories of estates in Scotland, which (unlike their English counterparts) never ceased to be publicly available. Annual Calendars of Confirmations of Estates, giving the names of the deceased, the trustees, and the total value of the estates and any additions to the original estate, were published by H.M. Stationery Office. There have been some interesting studies using this source, notably by W.P. Kennedy and Rachel Britton, into the structure of investment portfolios and their performance.[20] Such investigations are hampered by the information available in the inventories, which provides the name of the stock, the number of shares and their nominal value and the valuation at the time of death. For publicly quoted securities a value was fixed between the bid and offer price on the day of death. Other private stock was valued either according to certified and agreed prices provided by firms, or on the basis of performance over the previous three years determined by independent assessment.[21] The incautious have assumed that the nominal value of the share represented the actual cost of purchase. This is rarely the case. Shares, then as now, fluctuate in value and where a business was converted into a limited liability company or was taken over the subsequent share issues normally reflected some arbitrary valuation. The only way of determining how much was paid for individual stock is through personal investment records. Often when a business was organised as a partnership such transactions are recorded in the firm's financial records. This is the case for Peter Denny, senior partner of William Denny & Bros., shipbuilders at Dumbarton on the lower Clyde, from 1855 to his death in August 1895.[22]

The inventory of his estate given at Dumbarton in January 1896 revealed a fortune of £190,979.[23] This made him one of the twelve richest men to die leaving property in Scotland during the previous year according to calculations made by Rachel Britton.[24] The biggest estate was that of George Philip Stuart, Earl of Moray, who left nearly £853,000. Personal wealth on this scale was very unusual. Of the 6,742 people whose estates are included in the 1894 Calendar of Confirmations only 42 people left more than £100,000, and of those 20 had their principal residence outside Scotland.[25] The largest single fortune was that of the Duke of Sutherland, who left £1,275,088. Although he held vast estates in the north-east of Scotland, he drew most of his income from his valuable properties in the midlands of England. He was followed by Sir Archibald Orr Ewing, the textile magnate, with an estate of £1,077,234 and then by another non-resident, Lord Tweedmouth, with £714,861; next came a Glasgow engineer and locomotive builder, James Reid, with £677,624. Interestingly, despite the small number of these vast estates, they accounted for £10,165,810 out of a total for all estates of £23,937,481, some 40 per cent of all wealth-holding. Even fortunes at death of more than £10,000 were uncommon with only 385 of such estates, about five per cent in 1894.[26] However, together they account for more than £19.7 million, 75 per cent of all estates. This remarkable concentration of wealth in the hands of a very small group of people, less than 0.001 per cent of all deaths, is the context for the contemporary redistribution debate. However, with no reliable information about either the relationship of estates at death to total lifetime wealth holding or the dynamics of wealth accumulation and its place in the economy, the protagonists on either side could do little to advance their arguments. The analysis of an individual's lifetime financial transactions can begin to address these difficult questions.[27]

The accounting records that provide such information must be approached with caution, particularly if they cover a long period of time. Even if the physical appearance of the different series are the same and the numbering consecutive, there are sometimes changes in procedure. The content and style of entries may also change as partners and clerks came and went. Fortunately for the historian of the nineteenth century accounting practice of individual firms was extra-ordinarily enduring, often surviving takeovers and reconstructions. This continuity reflects the lack of legislation affecting either the way personal tax was assessed or the mode of reporting to shareholders.[28] Financial records were kept for the most part by bookkeepers, who had been trained within the firm for many years, usually being required to follow strict rules in posting entries.

The ledgers of William Denny & Bros. from the formation of the firm in 1844 until the end of the century are strikingly consistent. For example, a system introduced at the outset of balancing every quarter was maintained throughout, even though by the end of the century such a practice was outmoded. This resilience no doubt was largely due to Peter Denny's long career as senior partner from 1855 to his death in 1895. Born in 1821, the fifth son of William Denny, a shipbuilder in Dumbarton, Peter Denny was apprenticed at first to a lawyer in the town and then at the local glass works. At the age of 21 he joined his brother in the shipbuilding trade, gaining experience for a short period with the celebrated firm of Robert Napier & Sons in Govan. When his brothers established their own shipbuilding firm at Dumbarton in 1844 he became a junior partner using his commercial knowledge to organise the office. In 1850 he went into partnership with two engineers, John McAusland and John Tulloch, to form a marine engineering business that would function in harness with the ship-building enterprise. His eldest brother, William (after whom the shipbuilding company was named), died four years later, leaving Peter Denny virtually in sole command as his other brothers had more or less withdrawn from the partnership. Over the next 40 years, by investment in shipping companies, he built up a large business, specialising in small vessels for inland river navigation and long-haul vessels for routes to India and Australasia. Following the disruption in the Church of Scotland in 1843, Peter Denny had become committed to the Free Church of Scotland. This brought him into contact with the partners in the Glasgow shipping firm of Paddy Henderson & Co. with whom he collaborated in succouring the Free Church colony on the south island of New Zealand. He began to build ships for the Hendersons and took shares in their ventures, notably the formation of the Albion Shipping Co. in 1864. The following year he again joined with the Hendersons in the establishment of the Irrawaddy Flotilla Co. to provide shipping services to the interior of Burma. Eighteen years later they attempted a similar undertaking in the Argentinian and Uruguayan river systems, known as the La Platenese Flotilla Co.[29]

Details of Peter Denny's personal investment in William Denny & Bros., shipping companies, and other ventures are contained in his own account in the firm's ledgers. Every entry is dated, specifically described, and the amount given. These are the raw material for the investigation of the dynamics of the creation of his fortune during his lifetime. As a first step all his transactions, debits and credits, were entered into a simple flat file database, mirroring the original entries as precisely as possible. No attempt was made to corrupt the integrity of the clerk's work, no matter how idiosyncratic, or occasionally incorrect it may have appeared. As this work progressed it became clear from the detail recorded that the accounts included transactions far beyond the core business. For example, the purchase and sale of horses for himself and his sons was included and repairs to household furniture. Altogether 3,777 records were created. These were then manipulated by sorting, string searching and matching routines to bring together records that had similar descriptive entries, whether debits or credits.

At this stage it was possible to address the problem of classifying the entries by type. The typology that was used emerged naturally from the data, no attempt being made to impose a predetermined structure derived from presupposed models of behaviour in order to simplify analytical problems. For example, all the entries that related to shipping investments were classified in one group with sub-codes for individual ventures; similarly all entries relating to dividends from shipping investments were allocated to a common group. Where, as in these cases, the two groups related to each other, the sub-codes used in each were identical for convenience in subsequent analysis. For example, investment in the Rivers Steam Navigation Co. was code 0729, 07 for shipping investment, 29 for the company; the dividend income was coded 0829, 08 for shipping dividends and 29 again for Rivers Steam Navigation Co. Twenty-three different types of transactions were identified:

    01 Cash transactions
    02 Investments in William Denny & Bros.
    03 Profit and Loss on investment in William Denny & Bros.
    04 Withdrawal of capital from William Denny & Bros.
    05 General Investments
    06 Income from general investment
    07 Investment in shipping
    08 Income from shipping
    09 Expenditure on property
    10 Income from property
    11 Loans
    12 Loans repaid/interest
    13 Fees – directorships, etc.
    14 Underwriting account
    15 Business expenses
    16 Miscellaneous expenditure
    17 Miscellaneous income

18 Miscellaneous credit payments
19 Capital transfers to family
20 Charitable donations
21 Legacies
22 Investments sold
23 Shares in ships sold

Not all transactions could confidently be allocated to specific types, principally because the descriptions in the ledger entries were not sufficient. This was particularly the case for a large number of trivial transactions which probably related to household expenditures and the sale of garden produce.

When complete, a typical entry would appear in this format:

RENO (record number)	1588
DATE	1885 05 28
AMNT (amount in £s)	307.12
NOTR (nature of transaction)	Rivers Steam Navigation Company
TYPE (code group/sub-group)	0829

The database was then ready for investigation. In any analysis of such data there is the ever present danger of double counting, particularly through the mistaken assumption that all positive transactions represent income and all negative transactions was expenditure on investments. This is demonstrably not the case – some positive transactions will be the repayment of expenses incurred in the course of business and some negative transactions will be such expenses and consumables. To avoid this pitfall, if there was any doubt as to the nature of a transaction, it was placed in the miscellaneous groups 16 and 18.

Since both the contemporary and current historical debate has focused on the process of wealth creation, the first question to answer was from where did Peter Denny derive his income. Surprisingly, only 60 per cent of his total lifetime earnings came out of the shipyard and engine works (Figure 1). His shipping investments yielded him a further 40 per cent and the rest was made up of dividends on other investments, rents from property, interest on loans made to individuals, capital gains on investments, and director's fees. This suggests that even if investments were made by men like Peter Denny to bring work to their core business or secure supplies of raw materials, they were always expected to earn a return. Not unexpectedly the volume of this other income increased towards the end of his career. His earnings from William Denny & Bros. were composed of interest on his capital in the business and his share of the profit or loss for the year. These fluctuated markedly, reaching a first peak in 1855, followed by a sharp upturn between 1863–65 when the company was engaged in building blockade runners for the Confederate States. Despite another upswing in the early 1870s and in the mid-1880s, the total for 1865 was never exceeded. Nevertheless, for the next 25 years, with only four exceptions, he earned more than £10,000 a year from the company. Altogether he received more than half a million in income from the business. As in most partnerships, much of this was reinvested in the firm, providing the capital necessary for growth.

FIGURE 1

PETER DENNY: SOURCES OF INCOME 1844–95

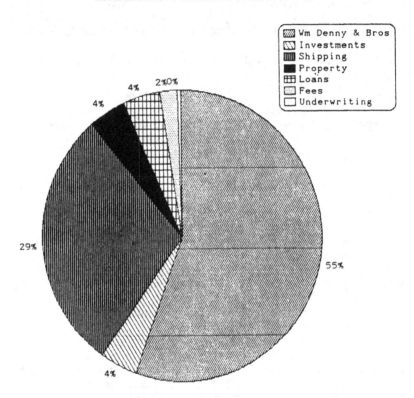

Peter Denny did not begin buying into shipping until 1853, with a modest investment of £20, in the *William Denny*, whose engineers were supplied by the engine works, but whose hull was built by a separate shipbuilding concern owned by his second brother, Alexander. His first large venture was in 1855/56, when he invested £11,500 in the *Zouave* (built as a speculation and sold on the stocks to Soloy Amat & Co.), purchased the old steamer *Beaver* from G. & J. Burns as part payment for a contract, and took a half stake in the *Italian* whose engines were supplied by Tulloch & Denny.[30] It was to be another decade before Peter Denny made another substantial investment when, in 1868, he put £12,000 into new ships under construction and entered into two joint ventures with the Hendersons,[31] purchasing shares in the Albion Shipping Co. to a value of £31,000 and in the Irrawaddy Flotilla Co. to a value of £8,000. His next big investments were in the mid-1870s when he was again deeply involved with the Hendersons, putting a further £5,000 into the Albion Shipping Co., £10,000 into Irrawaddy, and £25,000 in the newly-formed British and Burmese Steam Navigation Co. There were other peaks in 1881/2 and 1886. Altogether, during his career, he took shares in no less than 50 individual ships or shipping companies, totalling some £227,000. Peter Denny's largest investments were in ventures with Hendersons Irrawaddy Flotilla Co., accounting for over half the total. Altogether these investments in shipping earned him just over £280,000 in interest and dividends, an impressive yield quite apart from the business it brought to the yard (Figure 2).

FIGURE 2
PETER DENNY: EXPENDITURE, INCOME AND REVENUE
FROM GENERAL INVESTMENTS

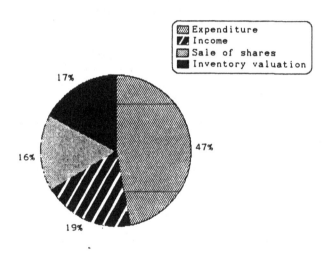

Expenditure	102992
Income	42260
Sale of shares	35760
Inventory valuation	37750

Not all the shipping investments were designed to be long term. Some were sold within a few months of purchase. During his career he disposed of shipping investments totalling £119,236, including sizeable holdings in Irrawaddy and Albion. Some of these transactions yielded handsome capital gains. The stake in the *Zouave* bought in 1855/56 for

£11,000, was sold the following year for £13,734 and the *Beaver* purchased from G. & J. Burns for £7,000 in the same year also sold in 1857 for £8,200. Albion stock to the value of £40,500 was re-purchased at a premium by the company in two tranches in 1871/72, and between 1882 and 1885. Although only to be expected, such capital transactions further complicate interpretation of the dynamics of wealth and calculations of total wealth creation.

It is difficult to relate the income from his shipping investments precisely to individual share purchases because some of the interest and dividends were derived from companies that had issued him stock on acquiring vessels in which he had previously held shares. Where it is possible to match investment to dividend/interest, notably in the case of the joint ventures with Hendersons, there is a pattern of little return in the early years and then a steady flow of income. Albion produced relatively little between 1868 and 1872, less than one per cent per annum over all. Thereafter returns vary between three and six per cent until 1892 (Figure 3). Irrawaddy followed a similar pattern but with much more impressive yields, once as high as 19 per cent of his total shareholdings. One of these shipping ventures with the Hendersons was an acknowledged disaster – the acquisition of the La Platanese Flottilla Co. in 1886, due to a combination of misfortunes – revolution, inflation and drought – the company incurred huge losses.[32] On a personal investment of £42,000, Peter Denny only received an income of £1,556. When the concern was finally liquidated in 1890, Peter Denny lost the whole of his investment and since there were insufficient funds to pay the secured loans of the debenture holders, the family company, William Denny Bros., agreed to split this obligation with Hendersons. Making a virtue out of a necessity, Peter Denny, as he lay on his deathbed, agreed to write off this loss amounting to over £88,000 against his shareholding in the business. As a result, in the valuation of the estate his share in William Denny Bros. was valued at a meagre £21,702. It is a measure of the success of these shipping investments that he was able to take such a massive reverse, which led to the suicide of his eldest son, William Denny III, in his stride.

Apart from his involvement in shipping, Peter Denny held a wide portfolio of other investments totalling, during his lifetime, £302,992 in 38 different concerns (Figure 4). Some of these were designed to secure supplies of materials to the yard, such as investments in the Consett Iron Co., Dennystoun Forge at Dumbarton, Steel Co. of Scotland, and the North British Railway. Some arose out of his association with the Hendersons and the Free Church, like the New Zealand Agricultural Society, New Zealand Preserving Co., New Zealand Grain Agency, Rangoon Oil Co., Burmah Oil Co., and Free Church Insurance Society. Some reflected local concerns and problems, like the Helensburgh Workmen's Public House Co. and the Glasgow Public Halls, and some were simply good investment opportunities, notably his involvement in the formation of the Rio Tinto Co. This was his largest

FIGURE 3
PETER DENNY: EXPENDITURE, INCOME AND REVENUE
FROM SHIPPING INVESTMENTS

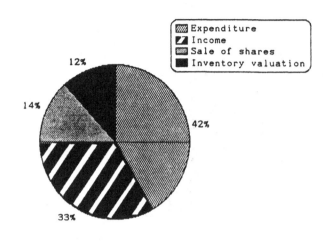

Expenditure	358097
Income	283406
Sale of shares	119235
Inventory valuation	100313

single venture outside shipping with an investment of £40,000 between 1873 and 1876. These investments, some of which were clearly made with charitable intent, appear not to have performed as well as those in shipping, yielding, all told, some £42,000 in his lifetime. However, almost 35 per cent of the total was sold between 1876 and 1880. The bulk of these sales were made in 1879 when he placed six parcels of his Rio Tinto shares on the market, netting a 15 per cent capital gain, some £3,000.

In assessing the performance of investment in companies, it is easy to forget that they sometimes generate other income in the form of director's fees. Peter Denny was chairman or a director of 12 companies in which he held shares, mostly concerns connected with the Hendersons. These included P. Henderson & Co. itself, Albion, Irrawaddy, British & Burmese Steam Navigation Co., and Rio Tinto. During his career he earned almost £20,000 in director's and other fees. The largest contribution came from Irrawaddy which paid him a total of £8,000 as chairman.

Like all his contemporaries in the West of Scotland, Peter Denny was involved in the property market, both to provide a home for himself

FIGURE 4
PETER DENNY: EXPENDITURE, INCOME AND REVENUE
FROM GENERAL INVESTMENTS

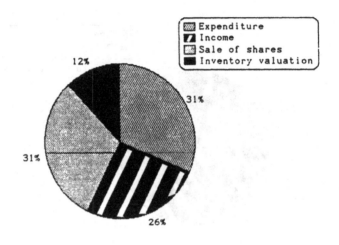

Expenditure	41599
Income	34384
Sale of shares	40507
Inventory valuation	15900

and also for others, particularly members of his staff and workforce. He also used his personal transactions to purchase property and plant for his firm. A simple balance of his property-related transactions shows that he spent £47,118 between 1845 and his death, receiving in income from rents and sales £41,162 (Figure 5). His property holdings at death included the mansion house he had built at Helenslee, various cottage and villa properties, and agricultural ground. His largest single transactions were reserved for his business – in 1862 he purchased the ground and plant used by the shipbuilding firm owned by his brother Alexander Denny for £9,746, retaining this until his death. His brother had got into financial difficulties at the time of the collapse of the Glasgow-based Western Bank in 1857 and his yard had closed two years later. In 1866 Peter Denny purchased a new yard and buildings for William Denny & Bros., itself, on the Leven for £9,600; in the following year, when the business had been transferred to the new site, he received payment from the firm for the yard, at £6,083 16s. the exact sum he had paid a year earlier, but not for the buildings (valued in 1866 at £3,517) which he retained (Figure 6). Four years earlier Denny had spent £3,293 on 'artizan properties' at Dennistoun to house workers. These dwellings entailed annual expenditure for repairs and insurance between 1863 and 1878 of up to £180; rents were around £420 per annum. From 1878 these properties no longer appear in the ledgers, nor is there any entry that can be attributed to their sale. Other workers' accommodation owned by Denny included the Norfolk Cottages, bought from Paddy Henderson & Co. for £1,122 in 1866 and sold in 1871 for £900.

FIGURE 5

PETER DENNY: MAJOR SOURCES OF INCOME FROM PROPERTY

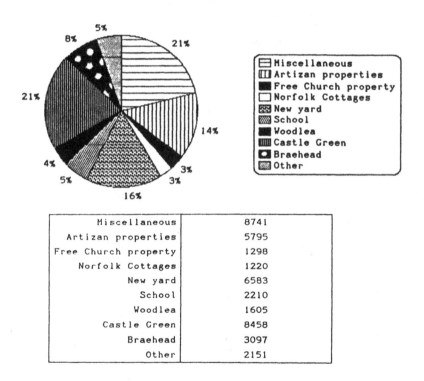

Miscellaneous	8741
Artizan properties	5795
Free Church property	1298
Norfolk Cottages	1220
New yard	6583
School	2210
Woodlea	1605
Castle Green	8458
Braehead	3097
Other	2151

Denny began the construction of his own home on the estate of Helenslee, some 43 acres looking out across the Clyde to the West of Dumbarton with an annual value of £2,014, in the spring of 1866.[33] The accounts suggest that work was not completed until summer 1868, by which time the cost of construction had reached some £9,980. This included both excavations and construction, the laying out of roads, the installation of a heating system, and the erection of a fern-house. Denny also spent heavily on the construction of a villa at Braehead for

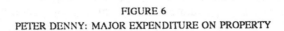

FIGURE 6
PETER DENNY: MAJOR EXPENDITURE ON PROPERTY

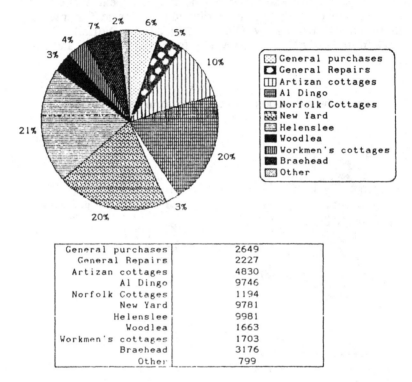

General purchases	2649
General Repairs	2227
Artizan cottages	4830
Al Dingo	9746
Norfolk Cottages	1194
New Yard	9781
Helenslee	9981
Woodlea	1663
Workmen's cottages	1703
Braehead	3176
Other	799

his son Archibald, who eventually purchased it from his father. Peter
Denny used his land in Dumbarton to provide a site for the building of a
manse for the minister of the local Free Church; this property was sold
between 1863 and 1866 realising some £1,200. He received throughout
his life a variety of miscellaneous payments of rents and feu duties on
property let out for grazing in the vicinity of his house and works – some
large sums under this heading, such as 'Sundries, buildings' in 1863, a
credit totalling £4,700, have not yet been fully explained.

Participation in the Dumbarton property market by Peter Denny
was part and parcel of his involvement in the local economy and
community. This found expression not only through the purchase of
equity in companies formed to provide benefit to local industry or
the community, but also, and more commonly, through loans to
individuals. During his lifetime he advanced cash to 49 organisations or
individuals, the majority connected to Dumbarton and the Clyde
shipbuilding and marine engineering industry. For example, he
advanced £4,000 to Robert Napier & Sons, when this firm got into

difficulties after 1885.[34] Altogether he loaned at least £50,000 during his lifetime, the largest advance was £5,000 to Alexander Crerar and the smallest £200 apiece to T. McNicol and H. Campbell, local tradesmen. From the information in the ledgers it is not always possible to distinguish loans from other transactions and where there was any doubt these were allocated to group 16 miscellaneous expenditure. Similarly, the source of interest on loans is not always clearly identified. As a result it is not possible to calculate his total lifetime profit from this source, but it seems likely that it may have been as much as £10–15,000. His willingness to act as a source of credit for sometimees substantial sums, confirms the impression gained from other sources that, until at least the First World War, the well-off were deeply committed to the finance of small enterprises either related in some way to their core business or to the communities in which they lived.

A few of Peter Denny's loans were to local charitable bodies and non-profit making companies like the Free Church North and the Dumbarton Building Co. More commonly Peter Denny gave directly of his fortune to support voluntary bodies. His ledger entries contain 13 charitable transactions, including £500 to the Glasgow Western Infirmary in 1873, £250 to the Royal Scottish National Institution for Mental Defectives at Larbert in 1874, £1,000 to the Glasgow Home for Incurables in 1875 and £3,300 to establish a bursary fund in the same year. Altogether these charitable donations amounted to £8,742 between 1870 and 1888. They are patchy; there are no recorded gifts in 1876 or 1879, between 1880 and 1882, and from 1889 to his death. From other recorded evidence of his charitable giving, for example, his public gift with John MacMillan of Levengrove Park in Dumbarton in 1885, it is clear that these transactions do not represent his total lifetime giving. Other donations, particularly those to Free Church causes, must have been made privately, outside the firm, from the cash sums he drew regularly from the business to meet his household and other expenses. Some of these expenses are referred to in his will when making provision for his wife to keep Helenslee going. He calculated she would need £3,000 a year to meet her expenses, including the gardener 'to upkeep the policies and garden'.

His net cash drawings fluctuated, but from 1871 there were only five years, apart from the year of his death, when he took out less than £10,000. His net drawings regularly exceeded £20,000, and in 1877 totalled just over £45,000, and in the three years 1883, 1884 and 1885 combined, the huge sum of £155,990 (Figure 7). Altogether he drew £604,322 in cash out of the firm in his lifetime. Such a vast sum cannot have been required solely for his domestic expenditure, but there is no way of telling precisely how it was dispersed. Since all the assets included in his inventory, with the exception of his household furnishings valued at £6,098, can be traced through his account with the firm, the larger part of all this cash must have been passed on as *inter-vivos* gifts to his eight children and in charitable giving. Although there is a

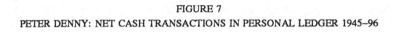

FIGURE 7

PETER DENNY: NET CASH TRANSACTIONS IN PERSONAL LEDGER 1945–96

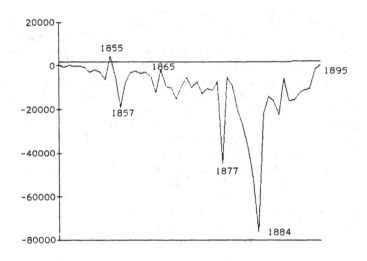

total of £32,000 in gifts to his children and other relatives between 1866 and 1892 contained in his transactions, this was by no means all the money that he passed on before his death. It is almost certain that the large withdrawals in 1877 and between 1883 and 1885 were to allow his sons to invest in Irrawaddy and La Platenese. The size of such gifts to his children can be gauged from the estate of William Denny III, who committed suicide at the age of 39 in 1887, leaving a total of £114,180. Only £1,910 of this sum can be traced as *inter vivos* gifts from Peter Denny through his father's ledger transactions.

There is enough evidence from the investigation of the financial transactions of other shipbuilders to be certain that Peter Denny's behaviour was typical of successful men in the industry. The detail contained in his firm's ledgers has allowed a level of scrutiny not possible for most of his contemporaries for the whole of their business careers. This reveals an extensive deployment of resources around the core business almost from the outset, designed not only to secure contracts, materials and services, but also to yield returns to allow for further integration. This dynamic view of a nineteenth-century entrepreneur is far removed from the two popular misconceptions of either the absentee rentier or the ever-present Gradgrind whose sole pre-occupation was the central manufacturing activity. To be certain that this picture is representative of the economy as a whole, further detailed case studies will have to be painstakingly compiled, particularly for the commercial sector and for landed proprietors. This will depend on the location of further continuous runs of business books with similarly detailed entries covering the partners' financial transactions outside the core activity of the company. There is no doubt that such series exist in archives throughout the United Kingdom, perhaps containing vastly more lifetime transactions than Peter Denny's. Their analysis will allow the debate amongst historians and economists about the function of wealth to advance into the crucial territory of accumulation and dissipation. At a time when governments throughout the world, both East and West, are seeking to encourage personal wealthholding, there can be few other historical questions with such contemporary relevance.

University of Glasgow

NOTES

1. Benjamin Disraeli, *Sybil* (London, 1845), p.31.
2. The best known of these collections is Samuel Smiles, *Men of Invention and Industry (London, 1884), Memoirs and Portraits of One Hundred Glasgow Men* (Glasgow, 1885) and for some Scottish examples, see the useful but not exhaustive list in Peter Bell, *Who was Who in Victorian Scotland* (Edinburgh, 1986), pp.4–5.
3. *The Grocer*, 18 Dec. 1897, pp.1464–5.
4. Ibid.
5. See, for example, letter from Kirkman Finlay to his son Alexander Struthers Finlay quoted in Colm Brogan, *James Finlay & Co. Ltd., Manufacturers and East India Merchants 1750–1950* (Glasgow, 1951), p.128 – 'You will know that there is nothing advances a mercantile man so much as character and this is to be obtained not only by the greatest attention, industry and regularity of conduct, information and intelligence in business, but also by that friendly and obliging disposition of mind and behaviour which wins the good opinion and interest of all by whom you are surrounded'.
6. D.W. Thompson, *Inquiry into the Principles of the Distribution of Wealth most Conducive to Human Happiness* (London, 1824), p.259.
7. Robert Giffen, 'Accumulations of Capital in the United Kingdom in 1875–85', *Journal of the Statistical Society*, Vol.LIII (1890), pp.1–35; William J. Harris and Rev. Kenneth A. Lake, 'Estimates of the Realisable Wealth of the United Kingdom Based Mostly on the Estate Duty Returns', *Journal of the Royal Statistical Society*, Vol.LXIX (1906), pp.709–32; Bernard Mallet, 'A Method of Estimating Capital Wealth from the Estate Duty Statistics', *Journal of the Royal Statistical Society*, Vol.LXXI (1908), pp.65–84; Robert Giffen, *The Growth of Capital* (London, 1889), *passim*.
8. Draft report to the Income Tax Committee, 1861, quoted in L.G. Chiozza Money, *Riches and Poverty* (3rd ed., London, 1906), p.12.
9. Discussion on Mr. Bernard Mallet's Paper, *Journal of the Royal Statistical Society*, Vol.71 (1908), p.96.
10. L.G. Chiozza Money, *Riches and Poverty* (3rd ed., London, 1906), pp.42, 52.
11. Ibid., pp.203–5.
12. F.W. Headley, *Darwinism and Modern Socialism* (London, 1909), pp.219–31.
13. Samuel Smith, *My Life and Work* (London, 1902), p.521.
14. J.G. Lockhart, *Cosmo Gordon Lang* (London, 1949), pp.239–40.
15. William Smart, *Second Thoughts of an Economist*, (London, 1916), p.102.
16. William Smart, 'New Wealth: A Study of the Source of Income', *Political Science Quarterly*, Vol.9 (1894), p.464.

17. R.S. Surtees, *Mr. Facey Romfords Hounds* (London, 1867), p.166. This view is confirmed in real life in the advice offered to John Denny on his marriage by his brother William Denny III in November 1883: 'Will you allow me to offer you one maxim which I have already offered to Archie and have acted on myself: "Never let your wife know your business"? Beyond knowing that I am a partner in the yard and engine-works, Lelia knows nothing. There are many reasons for this advice, but the principal is that in almost all disruptions of copartnership among brothers the cause is to be found in the jealousy of their wives, and not of themselves'. A.B. Bruce, *The Life of William Denny Shipbuilder* (London, 1889), p.99.
18. See the remarks of W.D. Rubinstein in *Men of Property: The Very Wealthy in Britain since the Industrial Revolution* (London, 1981) p.11.
19. See, for example, W.D. Rubenstein, 'British Millionaires, 1809–1949', *Bulletin of the Institute of Historical Research*, Vol.XLVII (1974), pp.202–23.
20. Rachel Britton, 'Wealthy Scots', *Bulletin of the Institute of Historical Research*, Vol.LVIII (1985), pp.78–9; W.P. Kennedy and Rachel Britton, 'Portfolio Behaviour of Economic Development: the Evidence from Scottish Probate Inventories' (unpublished discussion paper, 1982).
21. G.M. Green, *The Death Duties* (London, 1947), pp.258–60. An interesting account of this process, pre-1894, is contained in Allan Edwards, 'Probate Accounts', *The Accountant Students' Journal*, Vol.2 (1884), pp.395–7.
22. Glasgow University Archives (GUA), Business Records Collection, UGD 3/2/1–12, Ledgers of William Denny Bros. 1844–96.
23. Scottish Record Office, SC65/43/31.
24. Rachel Britton, 'Wealthy Scots, 1876–1918', *Bulletin of the Institute of Historical Research*, Vol.LVIII (1988), pp.111–94. There are some curious discrepancies about the lists of wealthy Scots included in this article. Although it is stated on pp.787 that the ten largest estates confirmed before Scottish courts were abstracted by hand from the Calendar of Confirmations, the lists do not seem to include people resident in England who had estates confirmed in Scotland. For example, in the list for 1894 the lowest estate in the listed top ten was £222,106 whereas there were 16 estates greater than this recorded in the Calendar. Amongst those omitted by Rachel Britton are some who were of Scottish descent with business interests in Scotland – Arthur Hutchinson, John Pearson Kidston, and Dudley Coutts Majoribanks, Lord Tweedmouth.
25. A database has been created of all estates contained in the Calendar of Confirmations for 1894 by the Archives and the Department of Scottish History at the University of Glasgow as part of an investigation into wealth-holding in Scotland in the late nineteenth century.
26. There are considerable doubts about the veracity of the valuations in the Calendar, see N.J. Morgan and M.S. Moss, 'Listing the Wealthy in Scotland', *Bulletin of the Institute of Historical Research*, Vol.LIX (1986), pp.189–95.
27. See for example N.J. Morgan and M.S. Moss, 'Urban Wealthholding and the Computer', in Peter Denley, Stefan Fogelvik and Charles Harvey (eds.), *History and Computing 2* (Manchester, 1989); M.S. Moss, 'Wiliam Todd Lithgow: Founder of a Fortune', *Scottish Historical Review*, Vol.LXII (1982), pp.47–72.
28. M.S. Moss, 'Forgotten Ledgers, Law and the Business Historian: Gleanings from the Adam Smith Business Record Collection', *Archives*, Vol.XVI (1984), pp.354–75; and C.W. Nobes and R.M. Parker, 'Chronology of the Development of Company Financial Reporting in Great Britain', in T.A. Lee and R.H. Parker (eds.), *The Evolution of Corporate Financial Reporting* (London, 1979), pp.197–202.
29. For a further account of Peter Denny's career, see Anthony Slaven & S.G. Checkland, *The Dictionary of Scottish Business Biography* (Aberdeen, 1986), Vol.1, pp.214–17; Paul L. Robertson, 'Shipping and Shipbuilding, the Case of William Denny and Brothers', *Business History*, Vol.XVI (1979), pp.36–47, and D.J. Lyon, *The Denny List*, Part 4 (London, 1976), appendix viii.
30. Information about these ships from D.J. Lyon, op. cit.

31. For an account of these ventures and others with the Hendersons, see Dorothy Laird *Paddy Henderson – The Story of P. Henderson & Co: 1894–1961*, Glasgow (1961), Chs.I and XI; Alister Macrae and Alan Prentice, *Irrawaddy Flotilla* (Paisley, 1978), *passim*.
32. Slaven and Checkland (eds.), op. cit., biography of Peter Denny.
33. This valuation is taken from Parliamentary Papers, C.899 (1874), *Scotland: Owners of Lands and Heritages ... 1872–73 Return*, p.46.
34. An account of the firm's problems is contained in John R. Hume and Michael S. Moss, *Beardmore – The History of a Scottish Industrial Giant* (London, 1979), p.49.

BRITISH ENTREPRENEURS
IN DISTRIBUTION AND
THE STEEL INDUSTRY

By CHRISTINE SHAW

When the *Dictionary of Business Biography*[1] was first planned in the Business History Unit of the London School of Economics, an integral part of the project was to provide data for a computer-assisted analysis of entrepreneurs in England and Wales between 1860 and 1980. This analysis is now under way, and some of the first fruits of this work are presented here.

One of the main lines of enquiry in the analysis of the social background, education and career patterns of the entrepreneurs included in the *Dictionary of Business Biography*, is to investigate how these patterns vary among the businessmen in different industries. Here, those engaged in distribution will be compared with those in one of the major manufacturing industries, steel. Distribution has suffered some degree of neglect from business historians, and one consequence of this was the difficulty of identifying individuals to represent this sector in the *Dictionary*, and of compiling adequate biographies for those who were identified. The result was that just under ten per cent of the entries in the *Dictionary* were of subjects engaged in distribution, even including those like Sir Reginald and William Rootes, who were principally manufacturers, but who developed important distribution networks for their products.[2] All together 114 individuals in the *Dictionary* were identified for the purposes of this analysis as being engaged in the distributive trades, including men like the Rootes brothers; these will be referred to as Group A. The steel industry is, by contrast, one of the most intensively-studied industrial sectors in the British economy and there was little trouble in identifying subjects for inclusion in the *Dictionary*. For the purpose of this study, again men have been included for whom the production of steel was perhaps a subsidiary interest, though still an important one, men such as Sir Herbert Lawrence, who brought the steel interests of Vickers into the English Steel Corporation in 1929.[3] There are 73 men included in this group in this study; they will be referred to as Group B.

A third group of entrepreneurs from the *Dictionary* is compared with Groups A and B. Referred to as Group C, this is a random sample of 188 subjects from four of five volumes of the *Dictionary*, those covering the letters A to R, which was analysed in an earlier study which I presented to the Anglo-Japanese Business History Conference of 1986. The coding for some of the variables was changed after that study, as various improvements suggested themselves, so that it is not possible to use this group for comparison at all points in the following analysis.

For the purposes of analysis, all three groups are divided into four cohorts by date of birth. The number of individuals in each cohort of each group and the percentage of that group those individuals represent is set out here to enable the findings analysed using these cohorts to be put into better perspective. In particular, it should be borne in mind that the fourth cohort of each group is comparatively small, and that the first cohort of Group B constitutes nearly half the group.

TABLE 1
COHORTS BY DATE OF BIRTH

Cohorts	Group A	Group B	Group C	
Born before	23	34	55	Number in Cohort
1840	20.2	46.6	29.2	Percentage of Group
Born 1840-69	43	17	63	
	37.7	23.3	33.5	
Born 1870-99	36	17	58	
	31.6	23.3	30.9	
Born 1900	12	5	12	
or Later	10.5	6.8	6.4	
	114	73	188	Total in Group

I

When the occupations of the fathers of the three groups are analysed, it emerges that the entrepreneurs engaged in distribution (Group A) were appreciably more likely than the steelmen (Group B) to be the sons of fathers in the same trade. About half of Group A, 49 per cent, had fathers engaged in occupations falling within the SIC (Standard Industrial Classification) category XXIII, distribution, while only 22 per cent of Group B had fathers engaged in metal manufacturing, SIC category VI, though a further 12 per cent had fathers who were occupied in the manufacture of metal goods, including ships and vehicles, SIC categories X, XI and XII.

Since it may now be considered an established finding that most entrepreneurs did not come from relatively poor families, classifications such as that used by Charlotte Erickson in her classic study of men in the steel industry and the hosiery trades,[4] require revision. Her classification into four groups puts industrialists, bankers, professional men and farmers into one category, and retail traders, no matter on what scale their business might be, into the same social category as bookkeepers and clerks. This is not really appropriate for the twentieth century, however, when retail firms such as Sainsburys and Marks and Spencer are among the largest enterprises in the economy. Classifications used in other studies of groups of businessmen also tend to result in too large a proportion of the subjects being analysed falling into their top social classes, and tend to distinguish between levels of wealth, rather than sources of wealth.[5] Yet the separation out of businessmen from those engaged in other trades and professions is surely desirable, and the separation of those involved in manufacturing industry from those in other industrial fields could highlight different recruitment patterns for different sectors of the economy.

I have, therefore, devised the following classification of occupations and social groups, even though this means I cannot compare the social background of the entrepreneurs considered here with those in earlier studies.[6]

1 – industrialist (partner, owner, director, senior manager)
2 – landowner, farmer
3 – professional (doctor, lawyer, clergyman, teacher, consultant engineer, etc.)
4 – banker, merchant, retailer (for example, owner or senior manager of a department store or retail chain), other non-manufacturing businessman (for example, hotelier, shipmaster)
5 – clerk, foreman, etc.
6 – independent craftsman, small retailer
7 – craftsman employed by others, labourer

A comparison of the social backgrounds of the men from Groups A and B reveals some interesting differences. Of Group A, 44 per cent had fathers in category four, which includes merchants and large retailers, and a further 13 per cent fathers in category six, which includes small retailers. Comparing these findings with those for the classification of fathers' occupations by SIC category, it is evident that most of the fathers of Group A in categories four and six were indeed retailers. Only 11 per cent of Group A were the sons of industrialists. By contrast, 40 per cent of the steelmen of Group B had fathers who were themselves industrialists falling within category one, and only 16 per cent had fathers engaged in the non-manufacturing business activities of category four. Steelmen were nearly twice as likely to have fathers in the professions: 21 per cent did so, as compared with 11 per cent of

Group A. They were, however, much less likely than those in the distributive trades to have fathers in the lower social categories five, six or seven: only ten per cent did so, compared to 25 per cent of Group A. It appears then, that distribution did offer greater opportunities for men from comparatively humble backgrounds than did the steel industry, perhaps simply because it took much less capital to open a shop than to start up a steelworks. Yet even in this trade, which must have been one of the easiest of all industrial and commercial fields for an enterprising man of little capital and few connections to get started in, it is those from comparatively privileged backgrounds who are in a clear majority, further confirmation of how rarely the story of a successful entrepreneur is a tale of 'from rags to riches'.

II

Nor do immigrants figure as largely in these two groups as the popular mythology of entrepreneurs would have it. There were rather fewer immigrants, only five per cent, among Groups A and B, than among the general Group C, of whom ten per cent were born outside the British Isles. The majority of these immigrants, furthermore, were not fleeing from poverty or persecution abroad, and one of the five individuals in Group A born abroad, two the four in Group B, and six of the 17 in Group C, were born to British parents.

As one might expect, London[7] was the great centre of attraction for the distribution entrepreneurs: over half of them, 54 per cent, were active there, of whom 44 per cent were born there. Only two of the 29 individuals in Group A born in London were principally active outside it. The call of London was particularly strong for those born in the south-west, with eight of the 12 individuals born there going to the capital, and in the south-east, which also lost eight of its 12 sons in Group A to London. Half of the eight men in Group A born in Yorkshire and Humberside went to London; only three stayed in the region of their birth. The majority of the seven men born in the west Midlands also left, with three going to London and only two staying behind. The east Midlands, however, apparently offered more attractive opportunities, with five of the six men born there making their careers there, and five of the six men born in the north stayed in their home region, too. The majority, nine out of 14, of those born in the north-west stayed there, while three moved to London; the migrants were replaced by five coming from other regions, making the north-west, with 12 per cent of Group A, the next most important region of activity for this group of distribution entrepreneurs after London. All the regions, except East Anglia, recruited one or two from elsewhere. The only member of Group A born in East Anglia stayed there, and one of the three men born in Wales was the only member of Group A to make his career in the principality.

By contrast, only seven per cent of Group B made their career in

London, and seven of the eight steelmen born there moved out to make their way in other areas of the country. Surprisingly perhaps, most of the steelmen born in Wales, three of five, moved away as well, though ten men came from other regions to work there; 16 per cent of Group B were active in Wales all together. Half of the 14 steelmen born in the West Midlands made their career outside it, though the region attracted three others, making it the main region of activity for 14 per cent of Group B. Of the 17 active in Yorkshire and Humberside, 23 per cent of Group B, 11 were born there; only two men born in this region worked outside it. All five of those born in the north worked there, but the north also attracted 13 men from other regions; these 18 men who worked in the north constitute 25 per cent of Group B.

III

As a group, the steelmen were somewhat better educated than the entrepreneurs in distribution. Only six per cent of the steelmen are known to have had no secondary schooling (though information is lacking on the schooling of 14 per cent of the group), and three of the four individuals concerned were born before 1840, the fourth being born between 1870 and 1900. Of Group A, 11 per cent are known to have had no secondary schooling (information is lacking on the schooling of 18 per cent of the group), with five of the 13 individuals concerned having been born before 1840, three in each of the second and third cohorts, and two even in the fourth cohort born in or after 1900. The figure for the general group, Group C, was of the same order, nine per cent.

Attendance at a public school is not necessarily, of course, the guarantee of a good education; still, it is of interest that half of the fourth cohort of Group A went to a public school, while 22 per cent of the third cohort had done so, and less than ten per cent of those born before 1870. Of those of Group B born before 1840, 12 per cent went to public school, as did between 40 and 50 per cent of three succeeding cohorts of steelmen. Once more, Groups A and B range themselves on either side of the general group C, of whom 15 per cent of those born before 1840 attended public schools and between 21 and 29 per cent of those born thereafter. The men of Group A born before 1900 were most likely to attend other independent schools, schools of particular religious denominations, old-established grammar schools and the like, as 36 to 40 per cent of these cohorts did, but none of those born in or after 1900 did so. The proportions of steelmen attending such schools declined over the first three cohorts from 53 to 24 to 18 per cent, only to rise to 60 per cent in the fourth cohort. In this instance, Group A is closer to Group C, for which the proportion of each cohort attending these independent schools fluctuated between 33 and 42 per cent.

A substantial proportion of steelmen, 38 per cent, had some kind of formal education, mostly (27 per cent) at a university, with 16 per cent attending Oxford or Cambridge universities. Of the distribution entre-preneurs, 14 per cent attended a university, with ten per cent going to Oxford or Cambridge, and only one individual was educated at an institute of higher education other than a university. The proportion of Group A receiving higher education is thus markedly below that for Group C, which is 29 per cent, and that of Group B markedly above it. Those born in or after 1870 in both groups A and B were more likely to have some formal further education than those born earlier. Of Group A, under ten per cent of the first two cohorts did so, but 22 and 58 per cent of the third and fourth. For Group B, the proportions of the first three cohorts were 28, 53 and 61 per cent, with the trend being reversed in the fourth cohort, of whom 40 per cent received further education.[8]

About the same proportion over all of Groups A and B received some formal further education or training, such as an apprenticeship, while they were employed: 23 per cent of Group A and 25 per cent of Group B did so. Only two men in Group A and one in Group B gained further qualifications by private study in their own time while they were in employment. The proportion serving apprenticeships or receiving other formal training from their employer tended to decrease over time for both groups, more markedly in the case of Group A, in which it declined from 35 per cent of the first cohort to eight per cent of the fourth, while for Group B it declined from 27 to 20 per cent.

IV

Contrasts in the patterns resulting from an analysis of the early careers of the entrepreneurs in the three groups are less marked than for some of the variables considered so far. Some variations between the groups do emerge, however. As so many of Group A had fathers who were themselves in the distributive trades, it is not surprising that 40 per cent of them began their working life in their family firm, and a further ten per cent joined their family firm after a few years gaining experience in another company. This tendency was particularly strongly marked in the third cohort, of whom 47 per cent started with their family firm, and 17 per cent joined it after working for a while elsewhere. Of Group B, 30 per cent began their careers in their family firm, and five per cent came to it after working elsewhere. The proportions of Group C in these two categories are very similar to those of Group B, 30 and three per cent. While the same proportion of all three groups, 19 per cent, began their careers by serving an apprenticeship, Group A shows a different pattern from the other two. Those in Group A born before 1840 were more likely than their contemporaries in the other two groups to serve an apprenticeship: 35 per cent of them did so, as compared with 21 and 22 per cent of Groups B and C. But while the proportions of those beginning their careers in this way in Groups B and C remained roughly the same, between 20 and 25 per cent (apart from dips to 14 per cent in the second cohort of Group C and to 12 per cent in the third cohort of Group B), the figures for Group A decline steadily, from 35 per cent to nothing. Both Group A and Group B were less likely than the general sample, in each cohort, to begin their career by simply acquiring work experience in a firm with which their family had no links without gaining formal qualifications, as 34 per cent of Group C did, as against 19 per cent of Group A and 16 per cent of Group B. Very few of the steelmen born between 1840 and 1899, only six per cent, took this path. Those in distribution were marginally more likely to set up their own business within five years of beginning to work, but the proportion is still very small, only three per cent; none of the steelmen did this. Steelmen were, however, more likely, and those in distribution less likely, to enter business after acquiring working experience in other fields, such as the army or the law, the proportions of Groups A, B and C being five, 14 and seven per cent respectively. Between 20 and 29 per cent of the steelmen born after 1840 followed this career path.

Entrepreneurs in both the steel industry and in distribution were much more likely to hold a position of major responsibility in business in their twenties or even earlier than were those in the general sample. In all, 69 per cent of Group B and 53 per cent of Group C held positions of major responsibilty by the age of 30, while 71 per cent of Group A did so. Of the first, large, cohort of Group B, 85 per cent had been given major responsibility before the age of 30, as against 67 per cent of the first cohort of Group C. The proportions of the second and third cohorts in this category were much closer in these two groups, 59 and 56 per cent for the second, and 53 and 45 per cent in the third for Groups B and C respectively, though the gap widened again in the fourth cohort, between 40 and 17 per cent. The proportion of the first cohort of Group A in this category, 78 per cent, is not so high as for Group B, but for the three later cohorts it is persistently higher, with 70 per cent in the second, 75 per cent in the third and 58 per cent in the fourth cohorts. Similar proportions of all three groups were given their first major responsibility in their thirties: 24, 21 and 27 per cent of Groups A, B and C respectively. Comparatively few in each group had to wait until their forties: four per cent of Group A, seven per cent of Group B and 11 per cent of Group C.[9]

The age at which the steelmen attained their first position of major responsibility does not seem to have been much affected by their social background. None of the men in Group B whose fathers came from social categories five, six and seven[10] had to wait until their forties. Although two of the seven individuals concerned had to wait until their thirties, they represent about the same proportion of the sub-group as that of the whole group falling within this category. Perhaps surprisingly, a comparatively humble background may have been more of a drawback in this respect to those engaged in distribution. Only one of the 29 individuals (25 per cent of the group) with fathers in social categories five, six and seven had to wait until his forties, but a rather higher percentage of them than of the whole group, 39 per cent as against 24 per cent, had to wait until their thirties.

The way in which a man spent the early years of his career did have some effect on the age at which he attained his first major responsibility in business. Some delay for those who came into business after beginning their career in other fields would be expected, and this proves to have been the case, with half of this category in Group B and 60 per cent in Group A not holding such a position until their thirties, and a fifth in both groups not until their forties. For those in Group C, the delay was even greater, with 27 per cent having to wait until their thirties and 46 per cent until their forties. The great majority of those in Groups A and B who started work in their family firm were given major responsibility by the time they were 30, 84 per cent of Group A and 81 per cent of Group B; these figures are rather higher than for this category in Group C, 67 per cent. All of the steelmen and all but one of those engaged in distribution who began their career in another company before entering their family firm held a responsibile position by the age of 30.[11] Serving an apprenticeship, or studying for other qualifications could delay, not speed up, progress to responsibility. This is especially the case for Group A, of whom 46 per cent of those serving apprenticeships had to wait until their thirties, as did two of the four men who studied for other professional qualifications while working, while a third had to wait until his forties. In Group C, too, these categories lagged behind, with 35 per cent of apprentices and 82 per cent of those acquiring professional qualifications while working having to wait until their thirties or later. Apprenticeships for those in the steel industry were not quite such a brake on progress, for only 29 per cent of apprentices had to wait until they were 30 or older, and one of the two individuals who studied for other professional qualifications. Yet they still made slightly slower progress than those whose early careers were spent gaining work experience without formal qualifications in a firm in which their family had no interest, for 75 per cent of these gained responsibility in their twenties, as did 69 per cent of this category in Group A. Those in Group C in this category lagged behind all others except those who might have hoped to advance their career by acquiring professional qualifications, and those entering business later in life, for less than half, 48 per cent, gained major responsibility in their twenties.

Once a man had attained a position of responsibility in distribution he was very unlikely to move to another firm later: 87 per cent stayed where they were, while ten per cent moved once and only three per cent moved on more than once. There was no significant variation in this pattern over time. Steelmen were more prepared to move on, though 62 per cent stayed with the firm with which they attained their first responsible position for the rest of their careers, while 26 per cent moved once and 12 per cent moved more than once. With this group there was some variation in the pattern over time, those in the second cohort being less mobile, with 77 per cent not moving on, and the small fourth cohort being markedly more mobile, with only one of the five not moving on, three moving on once and the fifth more than once. In the general group, 78 per cent stayed where they were after being given major responsibility, 12 per cent moved once and ten per cent more than once, so the steelmen were more mobile than the general group and those in distribution less so. There does not appear to be any significant correlation between the age at which a man was given his first major responsibility and his mobility, or lack of it, to other firms later.

V

In order to explore the differences between types of entrepreneurs, that is, founders, inheritors and managers, the men in the groups were divided according to their relation to the firm with which they spent the most significant part of their career. Thus, those classified as founders could well have started work in their family firm, or been employed as a manager, before they struck out on their own and founded the firm with which they made their name. Founders also include those who bought their way into an established firm and built it up, and managers include those managers who subsequently became partners in the firms they worked for.[12]

Nearly half of Group A, 48 per cent, were founders, as were a third of both Group B and Group C. The similarity of the totals for Groups B and C conceals a very different pattern over time. In Group B, 56 per cent of those born before 1840 were founders; it should be borne in mind that this cohort is twice the size of any other in Group B, and thus in fact 79 per cent of all the founders in Group B were born before 1840. The remainder were born between 1840 and 1870, representing 29 per cent of that cohort, with no founders being born after 1870. The pattern among the general group was that about two-fifths of the first two cohorts, 42 and 41 per cent, were founders, and between a fifth and a quarter of the remaining cohorts, 21 and 25 per cent. The pattern among Group A was quite different, with about the same percentage of founders as in Group B among those born before 1840, 57 per cent, and an even larger proportion of those born between 1840 and 1869, 65 per cent. The third cohort still had a substantial proportion of founders, 36 per cent, but the fourth only eight per cent.

The proportion of inheritors in Groups B and C was again the same, about a third, and for this category the patterns over time matched each other more closely than for the founders. In Group B 27 per cent of the first cohort were inheritors, 41 per cent of the second and third cohorts and none of the fourth; in Group C, it was a third of the first two cohorts, 38 per cent of the third and eight per cent of the fourth. There was an increase, a fairly steep one, in the proportion of inheritors in Group A, from the 26 per cent of those born before 1870, to 56 per cent of those born between 1870 and 1899, with only a slight fall, to a half, among those born in or after 1900.

As there were more founders and inheritors among the distribution entrepreneurs than among the steelmen and the general group, there were obviously fewer managers among their ranks. Only 14 per cent of Group A were managers, as against about a third of Groups B and C. Starting with much the same proportion in the first cohort as Group B, 17 and 18 per cent respectively, Group A had less than ten per cent of managers in its middle cohorts, though 42 per cent of those born in or after 1900 were managers. The proportion of managers among the steelmen increased with each cohort, from 18 per cent of the first, to 29, 59, and, in the fourth cohort, 100 per cent. After holding steady for the first two cohorts at a quarter, the proportion of managers among Group C also rose, from 41, to 67 per cent of those born in or after 1900.

When the three types of entrepreneurs in Groups A and B are classified by the occupation of their fathers, it becomes evident that it was indeed easier for someone from a comparatively humble background to found a company in distribution than in the steel industry. Of those in Group A with fathers who were labourers or craftsmen employed by others, 82 per cent founded their own firms, as did 60 per cent of the sons of independent craftsmen and small retailers, a further 27 per cent of the latter group inheriting the business with which they made their careers. All of the three individuals whose fathers were clerks or foremen became managers, however. Of those who had more prosperous fathers in non-manufacturing business, including retailers and merchants, 72 per cent were inheritors, but 29 per cent founded their own firms and only six per cent were managers. All the sons of farmers and landowners were founders, as were just over half, 55 per cent, of the sons of professional men.

Among the steelmen, the sons of professional men largely became managers, two-thirds doing so, though a quarter were founders. Of the seven individuals with fathers in the lower social categories five, six and seven, few became managers, with one from category seven and one from category six becoming founders; the seventh inherited his business from a father in category five who set up on his own after his son's birth. The majority of the sons of landowners and farmers, 71 per cent, set up their own business, though two individuals inherited landed estates which included steelworks.

Of those with only elementary or primary schooling, the majority in Group A, 70 per cent, and half in Group B and C, were founders. Those who went to public school were less adventurous, though many inherited the business with which they made their careers, so had less incentive to found their own. Of Group A, two-thirds of those who went to major public schools[13] and 86 per cent of those who went to minor ones were inheritors, while in Group B half of those who went to major public schools were inheritors and 42 per cent became managers, as did 56 per cent of those who went to minor public schools, though a third of the latter group were founders. Formal further education did not encourage men to become founders, either: only five per cent of the large numbers of founders in distribution received such an education, 17 per cent of the founders in the steel industry and nine per cent of those in the general group. By contrast, about a third of the inheritors in Groups A and C and three-quarters of those in Group B had some formal further education, as did about half the managers in all three groups.

A rather higher proportion of those who started work in their family firms in distribution and the steel industry, 29 and 27 per cent respectively, became founders than the nine per cent of Group C who did so. Inheritors, predictably, tended to start their career with the family firm, as did 72 per cent of those in Group A, 61 per cent in Group B and 74 per cent in Group C. Although apprenticeships could delay advancement, they could be an effective preparation for founding one's own firm, as 77 per cent of the apprentices in Group A, 43 per cent in Group B and 49 per cent in Group C did, for there was a greater percentage of founders among the apprentices than for each of the groups as a whole. A man who began his career gaining work experience in a firm with which he had no family connections was, however, about as likely as one who served an apprenticeship to become a founder, as 64 per cent of those in Group A, and 50 and 46 per cent of Groups B and C, did.

In all three groups, managers tended to have to wait longer for their first position of real responsibility. Among the managers in distribution, 56 per cent had to wait until their thirties, and six per cent until their forties, while 79 per cent of inheritors and 76 per cent of founders enjoyed such a position in their twenties. In the case of the steelmen, 54 per cent of managers enjoyed major responsibility in their twenties, but 15 per cent not until their forties, while 70 per cent of inheritors and 83 per cent of founders held such posts in their twenties. Among the general sample, about a third of the managers, as against about two-thirds of inheritors and founders, were given major responsibility before the age of 30.

Once they had been given an important task in their family firm, inheritors in all three groups were very unlikely to leave, for 98 per cent of those in Group A, 96 per cent of those in Group B and 95 per cent in Group C stayed put. Managers were the most mobile, particularly in the steel industry: of the managers in Group B a third moved once after achieving a responsibile position and a further third moved at least once more. Of the managers in Group C, 21 per cent moved once and 18 per cent more than once, though those in Group A were rather less likely to move, with 19 per cent moving once and six per cent more than once. Founders in distribution were almost as likely as managers to move firms after achieving major responsibility, with 13 per cent moving once and six per cent more than once. About the same proportion of the founders in the general group moved on, 11 per cent once and a further

11 per cent more than once, while founders in the steel industry were, like managers in this group, particularly mobile, with 42 per cent moving once and five per cent more than once.

VI

The main features of the characteristic pattern of the careers of distribution entrepreneurs could be explained, in large part, by the fact that comparatively little capital was required for an individual to set up a business in the distributive trades, and that it was comparatively easy in this field for a successful businessman to generate sufficient funds from the business and his family resources alone to finance expansion. Retailing in particular gave scope to men to found their own business: 55 per cent of founders were retailers, or putting it another way, 59 per cent of all retailers were founders. Wholesalers were more likely to be inheritors, as 45 per cent of them were, representing 44 per cent of all inheritors.[14] From this pattern of capital requirement derives the high percentage of founders and inheritors among the ranks of the distributors, with founders continuing to appear in each cohort, and the higher percentage of those from the lower social ranks who were successful in this field. From the high incidence of family firms, comes the relative immobility of the entrepreneurs in distribution, as they stayed with their business and were often able to maintain family control of them.

The structure of the industry and its capital requirements are also reflected in the steel industry. There was a high percentage of founders in the early years of technical experiment and innovation in the nineteenth century. Then, as steel firms became fewer and bigger, or became part of large manufacturing groups by takeover, or by diversification, there were no more founders, for it was impossible for an individual, perhaps even for a group of men, to find the capital to set up a new steel firm to compete with the established ones. The size of the enterprises in the twentieth-century steel industry attracted recruits from more privileged backgrounds, with a better, or at least a more expensive, education than the average entrepreneur. But these men were not anything like as innovative as the earlier generations of steelmen had been. About a third of the steelmen were associated with technical innovation, either initiating it or fostering it, but only two of these were born in or after 1870, while eight of the 17 men born between 1840 and 1869 were associated with innovation in some way. Only two of those who went to university were, while of the seven inventors in the group, five had no formal further education. The leaders of the industry in the twentieth century seem to have been preoccupied above all with restructuring it: was their apparent lack of interest in technological innovation due to failure of imagination, or forced on them by circumstances?

The analysis of the social background, education and career patterns of these two groups of entrepreneurs indicates the potential of a full quantitative analysis of the subjects in the *Dictionary of Business Biography*, as a means of illuminating and helping to explain the history of businessmen and business in British society. To speak of British business recruiting from too narrow a range of social groups is perhaps to stand the problem on its head. Men choose industries, as much as, if not more than, industries choose men, and a man's choice of career is shaped by a range of factors, including family tradition, education,‾ community pressure, geographical factors and personal inclination. Building up a social profile of the leading figures in the various industrial and commercial sectors of the economy will help us to understand better the 'social history' of the businessman in British society, and how that history can help to explain the economic history of Britain.

Business History Unit,
London School of Economics

NOTES

1. David Jeremy and Christine Shaw (eds.), *Dictionary of Business Biography*, 5 vols. (London, 1984–86).
2. Ibid., Vol.4, pp.933–40.
3. Ibid., Vol.3, pp.667–74.
4. Charlotte Erickson, *British Industrialists: Steel and Hosiery 1850–1950* (Cambridge, 1959).
5. For example, Philip Stanworth and Anthony Giddens, 'An Economic Elite: A Demographic Profile of Company Chairmen', in Stanworth and Giddens (eds.), *Elites and Power in British Society* (Cambridge, 1974), in which they found that 66 per cent of their sample of 460 chairman of large companies between 1905 and 1971 were from the 'upper class', by which they meant industrialists, landowners and others possessing substantial wealth and property.
6. In my earlier study of the general group, Group C, I used Erickson's classification of occupations, so that my findings for that group cannot be used for comparison here.
7. The regions used here are the Standard Regions of England and Wales, defined before the revision of the county boundaries in 1974, and as used in the *Abstract of Regional Statistics* (HMSO, 1973).
8. This cohort is so small, only five individuals, that it would need only one more man to have gone to university for the proportion to have been maintained at the level of the third cohort.
9. The age at which they achieved major responsibility is not known for one, four and nine per cent of Groups A, B and C respectively.
10. See above, p.50.
11. It should be borne in mind that those who started work in their family firm did not always stay in it.
12. The variable for father's occupation codes the father's occupation at the birth of the subject. The father may have started up a firm after his son's birth, and consequently not all inheritors in Group A, for example, have fathers in categories four or six.
13. That is, the 'Clarendon schools', Charterhouse, Eton, Harrow, Marlborough, Merchant Taylor's, Rugby, St Paul's, Shrewsbury, Wellington, Westminster and Winchester.
14. 37 per cent of Group A were wholesalers, 45 per cent retailers, and 18 per cent engaged in both wholesaling and retailing.

INTERPRETING THE RECORD OF WAGE NEGOTIATIONS UNDER AN ARBITRAL REGIME: A GAME THEORETIC APPROACH TO THE COAL INDUSTRY CONCILIATION BOARDS, 1893–1914

By JOHN G. TREBLE

The coal industry conciliation boards were responsible for setting the absolute rate of wages for the majority of pits in the British coalfields during the period 1893–1914. The onset of war brought about a degree of government regulation of labour contracts, particularly in strategic industries, but prior to this collective bargaining proceeded from quarter to quarter largely undisturbed by governmental control, except for legislation concerning minimum wages in 1912, and hours of work in 1908. Throughout the period the structure of wage payments remained the same: workers were paid a piece rate per ton of coal produced, which was supplemented by the addition of a percentage. The piece rates were negotiated locally and differed from seam to seam; the percentage addition was negotiated at district (coalfield) level by the conciliation boards. An important determinant of the percentage was the price of coal, although in principle other factors could be brought into play. The majority of conciliation board agreements specified limits on the extent of this variation, which were effective in reducing the variability of miners' wage rates.[1]

The purpose of this article is to study the way in which the conciliation boards reached decisions. We do not study the wage or earnings outcomes produced by these institutions, but rather the operation of the wage bargaining machinery itself. The article is an exercise more in industrial relations history than in economic history, although the methods and motivation for the study are grounded in the economics literature. It is also preliminary to the extent that we have not yet investigated the empirical implications of the theory described here. This is reserved for later work.

The conciliation boards were joint committees of the Coal Owners' Associations and the Trades Unions. They were set up by mutual agreement following lengthy negotiations over what the rules should be. One feature of the records left by the boards is that despite the similarities in their constitutions, the way in which they operated differed markedly from board to board. One of the best contemporary studies of the coal industry conciliation boards is W.J. Ashley's book *The Adjustment of Wages* (1903). Ashley noted that the conciliation board in the Durham coalfield was extraordinarily successful in reaching negotiated (as opposed to arbitrated) decisions. Ashley says (p.76): 'In Durham, for reasons which are not apparent, and which can only be conjectured as personal, the two parties on the board since its reconstitution in 1899 have managed to agree on each of the long series of quarterly changes (all of which ... have been reductions since February 1901), without calling in an outsider'. This contrasts with the record of the other coalfields quite sharply.

The first task tackled in this paper is a summary of the record of the negotiations up to the start of the First World War. We are able to take advantage of 11 years further data than Ashley had access to. None the less, Ashley's observation survives. The remainder of the article attempts to argue that the observed incidence of negotiated and arbitrated settlements is explicable in terms far removed from the 'personal' conjectured by Ashley. We argue that the record is consistent with the predictions of a game-theoretic analysis of the rules of the various boards. In other words, the incidence of arbitrated settlements can be explained as the outcome of negotiators rationally exploiting the institutional rules within which they bargained.

In a companion article,[2] the wider issue of the construction of the rules themselves is addressed, and the use of the game theoretic ideas in this context is justified.

I

The data lying behind the present study are the verbatim records of the conciliation boards' negotiations over wage rates. They provide details of both arbitrated and negotiated settlements, and full sequences of offers and counter offers can be identified.

An unresolved issue in the theoretical literature is the question of the proportion of settlements within an arbitral regime that will be settled by arbitration, rather than by negotiations. Farber claims that this proportion can be predicted by observation of the size of a 'contract zone',[3] that consists of the set of negotiated solutions that are preferred by both parties to an arbitrated solution. The larger the contract zone, Farber claims, the larger the proportion of negotiated settlements will be. Crawford presents a counterexample of a bargaining situation in which a larger contract zone generates a smaller proportion of negotiated settlements.[4] One interesting feature of the coal industry's negotiations is the variance displayed in the observed proportion of arbitrated settlements. The relevant data are displayed in the second row of Table 1. Over the five bargaining units the proportion of arbitrated settlements varies from 57.14 per cent in South Wales, to 11.76 per cent in the Durham coalfield. In the continguous Northumberland coalfield the proportion is 56.60 per cent. The idea that the differences in experience can be explained by personal characteristics of the negotiators is difficult to support. Indeed, the Durham and Northumberland conciliation boards had some members in common.

They also had important differences in their rules that may be thought to have generated this widely divergent behaviour. In particular, the Northumberland arbitrator was always present at the negotiating sessions from the beginning, whereas the Durham constitution specified that the first meeting would take place without the arbitrator and if no agreement was reached, there would be an adjournment of the meeting. The reconvened meeting would include the arbitrator. This rule implied that the direct costs of arbitrating a settlement were considerably higher in Durham than in Northumberland, and we might therefore expect to observe a lower proportion of arbitrated settlements in Durham. Unfortunately, this argument does not hold much water either, because the South Wales arbitrator also had to be called in to a reconvened meeting, and this did not deter the Welsh negotiators from calling him in even more frequently than the Northumberland negotiators called in theirs. Furthermore, the direct costs of negotiations were tiny compared to the potential changes in the wage bill.

To summarise, the striking feature of the summary statistics in the first row of Table 1 is the large variation in the proportion of cases going to arbitration. The remainder of this article is an attempt to set up a theoretical structure within which this fact can be understood.

TABLE 1
SUMMARY STATISTICS

	Federated Area	South Wales	Scotland	Durham	Northumberland
Number of settlements under arbitral regime	23	28	30	51	53
Number of arbitrated settlements(%)	6 (26.09)	16 (57.14)	15 (50.00)	6 (11.76)	30 (56.60)
Mean spread of offers	2.80	3.19	3.00	5.40	2.10

Sources: National Library of Scotland (DEP 227/1–8, NF 791a).
Mitchell Library, Glasgow (338.272 Sco, TU 331.88122330942 MIN).
Northumberland County Record Office (NRO 759/35–37; NCB/C2/3–7).
Durham County Record Office (D/DCOMPA/ 135, 137; D/EBF 37; NCB/I/CO 67, 73; D/DMA 81).
University College of Swansea (H1–121; Hubert Jenkins 2–4; MFGB minutes).
National Union of Mineworkers, Sheffield (MFGB minutes).

II

The basis of the theory is a game theoretic analysis of the rules of the boards. These were agreed to by both parties and were recorded in writing as formal constitutions. They followed a common pattern with rules relating to the purpose and membership of the boards, frequency of meetings, procedures at meetings, chairmanship and voting rights, and the division of costs. The division of costs was always equal between the two sides, as was membership, although the sizes of the boards varied. These negotiation costs were small and for modelling purposes we ignore them. The voting rules were also uniform, ensuring that if there were to be a disagreement between the union and the owners, that this would result in a tied vote. Assuming solidarity on both sides of the negotiating table, the rules therefore constrained votes to be either unanimous or tied. In the event of a tied vote, procedures were carefully specified. In all the boards, the ultimate step in the procedures was the exercise of a casting vote by the chairman or umpire, who thus acted as an arbitrator. In all the boards except the Scottish board this final appeal to the arbitrator was also compulsory. In Scotland, it was necessary for both parties to agree to an appeal to the arbitrator.

One peculiarity of the wage setting arrangements that we shall refer to below is that the percentage additions were always made in multiples of predetermined percentage amounts. This implied that the possible offers and counter-offers also could only be made in terms of these quantities, thus restricting the negotiators to bargaining over a discrete set. The reason for this was to enable the workers to check that their pay was being calculated correctly. The percentages translate into monetary equivalents of 3d per shift (for example, Scotland) or 3d. (for example, South Wales) in the pound, and therefore depended on the units in which the piece rates were expressed. Thus, in Scotland, wage changes were always made in multiples of 6.25 per cent, while in South Wales they were always in multiples of 2.5 per cent.

The main source of differences between the constitutions lay in the course of events between an initial disagreement and an appeal to the arbitrator, and it is this fact that we use in this paper as the basis for our argument. The differences are of importance because they affect the strategic implications of various decisions by the parties. In particular, in some of the boards, there was an advantage conferred by the rules on a party who could cause a decision to be delayed, and a corresponding disadvantage conferred on the other party. The device by which the delay could be achieved was an appeal to the arbitrator, and the advantage arose because of the timing of settlements.

If a change in the wage rate was settled upon, the change would be effective in the next pay following the settlement, and not at any predetermined date. Since wage rates were determined largely by the price of coal under an arrangement called the 'sliding scale', this meant that a delay in the date of settlement was advantageous to the union when the coal price was falling, and advantageous to the owners when the coal price was rising. Accordingly, when the coal price was rising, the union had an interest in a quick settlement, while the owners had a similar interest when the coal price was falling.

This feature of the constitutions was not common to all the bargaining units. In Northumberland and South Wales, the timing of meetings was such as to make effective delay impossible. In the other jurisdictions, the rules were drawn up in such a way as to permit strategic delay.

The rules of the Northumberland board specified that the arbitrator would be present at every meeting, and would have a casting vote in the event of disagreement. This meant that any impasse could be resolved instantly by an appeal to the arbitrator. In South Wales, the arrangement was more complicated, but still ensured that strategic delay was unconstitutional. This was achieved by careful scheduling of the dates of meetings, with the final meeting in the longest allowable sequence taking place before the earliest possible date for the wage rate adjustment. This final meeting was convened with the arbitrator present and a solution to the impasse was thus guaranteed.

The theoretical problem that confronts us is that of modelling the behaviour of the parties negotiating under the constraints imposed by these rules. We take it as read that the appropriate techniques are those of game theory, which now forms the basis of economists' thinking about issues in bargaining and arbitration.[5] More controversial perhaps is the particular use that we make of these techniques. We adopt the view that the fundamental problem that has to be solved in any wage negotiation is the division of a rent between the two parties involved. The size of this rent is not known before the division of the rent, and *ex post* information about the size of the rent is probably asymmetric, in the sense that the employer usually is better informed about it than the employee. The history of wage negotiations in the coal industry, and particularly the evidence uncovered by the Sankey Commission in 1919, suggest that the assymmetry of information in the period we are considering was considerable. Costs and profits were closely guarded secrets, and their sizes could only be guessed at from evidence of publicly declared dividends. Despite the difficulties induced by these characteristics of the industrial relations environment, we can argue that the institutions that were agreed to by the two sides were probably well equipped to handle them.[6] If this argument is accepted, it implies that the whole of the institutional structure has the characteristics of a sequential equilibrium, and therefore that the final stage in the wage settlement procedure can be analysed using the Nash equilibrium concept. Most of the rest of this paper is aimed at doing this.

III

A game is any situation where the outcome depends on the behaviour of several individuals. The individuals are known as players, and the various possible choices of behaviour open to them are called strategies. It is also supposed that each player has some interest in the outcome of the game. This is called his pay-off. A game is described by the players involved, the strategies available to each, and the pay-off function which describes what each player receives when each possible combination of strategies is played.[7]

Apart from a description of the game being played by the two parties, we also need to have a method for solving the game. This usually involves an assumption of rationality on the part of the players. They play in such a way as to maximise their own pay-off from the game. The solution concept used in this article is the Nash equilibrium, which requires that each player chooses a strategy that maximises his pay-off, given the optimal strategy of the other player.[8] The idea of a Nash equilibrium can be thought of in several different ways. One way is to think of the Nash equilibrium as a particular set of strategies, one for each player, which if they were played would not cause either player to wish that he had played differently. That is, strategies form a Nash equilibrium if knowledge of the other players' actual behaviour would not cause a player to change his own behaviour. Another way of thinking of Nash equilibrium is in terms of best replies. For each strategy of Player A, we can possibly construct the best reply of Player B. This is the strategy (or set of strategies) that maximises Player B's pay-off, given that Player A uses the specified strategy. Similarly, for each strategy available to Player B, we construct the best reply of Player A. If both elements of a pair of strategies (one for each player) are best replies to the other, then the pair constitutes a Nash equilibrium.

The Nash equilibrium has a convenient graphical representation in terms of the best-reply function of each player. In Figure 1, we show a best reply function for Player A. On the horizontal axis is the set of strategies available to Player B. On the vertical axis is the set of strategies available to Player A. They are represented as a [0,1] interval in Figure 1 because in the games that are discussed later in the article, negotiation will be over how a rent should be shared. In these circumstances the strategies available to each player involve calling out a suggested share for himself, or equivalently for his opponent. The best replies of Player A to given strategies of Player B can be read off from the curve. Figure 2a shows best reply functions for both players in the same space. Since in a Nash equilibrium pair of strategies each is a best reply to the other, Nash equilibrium is indicated by the pair of strategies at which the best reply functions cross. We will use this graphical apparatus extensively in the remainder of the article.

Several important points need to be made about the idea of Nash

FIGURE 1
A BEST REPLY FUNCTION FOR PLAYER A

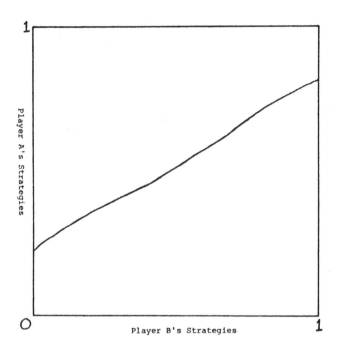

equilibrium. First, it is not necessarily the case that a Nash equilibrium will exist for any given game. (Figure 2b). Indeed, in certain degenerate cases the best reply functions themselves may not exist. Second, even if a Nash equilibrium does exist, it need not be unique. (Figure 2c). Third, the equilibria identified by this graphical technique are not the only equilibria that can exist. The equilibria characterised by the intersection of best reply functions are known as *pure strategy equilibria* because they involve the use of a single strategy by each player. Even if there is no pure strategy equilibrium, there will sometimes exist an equilibrium in *mixed strategies*. In a mixed strategy equilibrium players pick pure strategies at random, using a probability distribution over the strategies available to them. An equilibrium of this type is defined as a set of probability distributions, one for each player. If each player randomises his play according to his equilibrium distribution, he will receive an *expected* pay-off no less than the expected pay-off yielded by any other randomisation, as long as the other players also play their equilibrium strategies.

FIGURE 2a

NASH EQUILIBRIUM IN PURE STRATEGIES

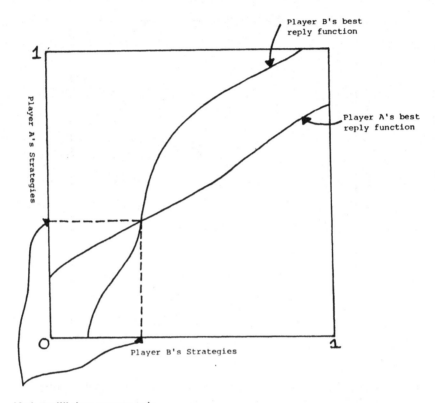

Nash equilibrium strategy pair

The argument in the next section takes the following form: we first formulate a game, the strategies and pay-offs of which we claim reflect in certain essential features the characteristics of the conciliation board proceedings and constitutions. This formulation is consistent with the premiss of a theorem of Dasgupta and Maskin[9] which proves that mixed strategy equilibria exist for games of this type. We then use the graphical technique to show conditions under which equilibria are of the pure strategy type. The importance of this distinction is that if the only type of equilibrium that applies is a pure strategy equilibrium, we would expect to see the same type of behaviour repeated in successive negotiations. For instance, the equilibrium might be such that it is always worthwhile for the parties to call in the arbitrator. If, on the other hand, the only equilibrium is a mixed strategy equilibrium, we would be able to explain behaviour that involves calling in the

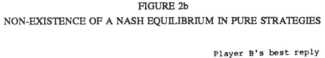

FIGURE 2b
NON-EXISTENCE OF A NASH EQUILIBRIUM IN PURE STRATEGIES

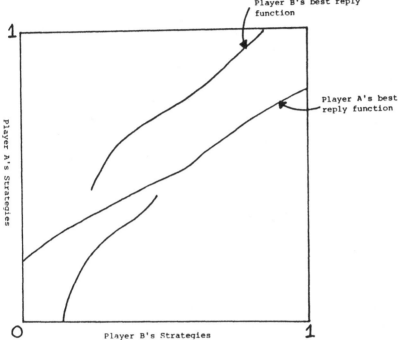

arbitrator on some occasions but not on others. We argue that if we ignore the discrete nature of the strategy set available to the coal-mining negotiators, then the boards with rules that exclude the possibility of strategic delay, should always call in the arbitrator,[10] because the only equilibrium under rules of this kind is a pure strategy equilibrium. In the boards that permit strategic delay, we would expect to see more varied behaviour, with the arbitrator sometimes being called in and sometimes not.

As it happens, the two boards with the highest frequency of appeal to the arbitrator (Northumberland and South Wales) are indeed those whose rules excluded the possibility of strategic delay. This fact provides some weak empirical support for our hypothesis. It does raise the question of why an appeal to the arbitrator was not made on every occasion. We suspect that this is because our model treats the strategy space as if it were continuous, when in fact negotiators were limited to making offers that were multiples of certain predetermined percentage amounts.

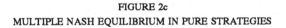

FIGURE 2c
MULTIPLE NASH EQUILIBRIUM IN PURE STRATEGIES

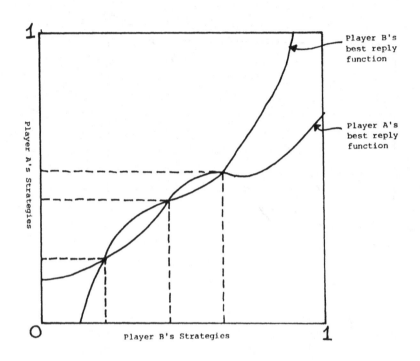

IV

In modelling the games induced by the rules of the conciliation boards, we will assume that there are only two players: the owners and the union. The strategies available to them are the various offers and counter-offers they might make as regards the percentage addition to the basic wage rate. We suppose that in making these offers they have in mind the division of a rent. The offers that they can make are bounded by the necessity of the owners to make normal profits, and by the existence of reservation wages for workers. If, given other costs and prices, the wage rate is set above the level that yields normal profits, the mines would not be profitable to run. If, on the other hand, wages were set below the level required to persuade the workforce to work in the mines rather than elsewhere, the mines would not be able to run. Because these bounds on the possible rates that can credibly be suggested exist, we regard the strategies available to the players as all possible divisions of this rent.

The specification of the game is completed by a description of the pay-offs. For each possible pair of strategies we have to describe what each party gets as the outcome of the negotiation. We here make the simplifying assumption that the pay-off to the union is higher *ceteris paribus* the higher is the agreed wage rate, and that the pay-off to the owners is higher, the lower is the agreed wage rate. Expressing pay-offs in terms of discounted future flows of benefits is cumbersome and adds unnecessarily to the complexity of the argument.

The form of the pay-offs will depend on whether there is agreement, or the arbitrator makes the decision. The specification is simple if both parties choose the same strategy. In this case, the parties agree and the outcome will be whatever the agreed division of the range happens to be. If the union asks for a higher wage than the owners offer, the arbitrator will be called in and the pay-off will be determined by whatever considerations the arbitrator deems to be important. In the present article we will follow Ashenfelter and Bloom[11] in writing the arbitrator's decision as a random choice between the final offers of the parties.[12] According to this model, since the offers have been decided the arbitrator's role is that of a simple coin-tossing machine. It is important to realise, however, that the arbitrator's presence will also influence the formulation of the offers. This assumption implies that the pay-off functions have the shapes indicated in Figure 3, as long as there is no cost (or benefit) attached to calling in the arbitrator.[13] To see why this is the case, note that the pay-offs are expressed as expected utilities derived from given pairs of offers and for each player the function is drawn conditionally on the offer made by the other player. Each pay-off function is in two sections separated by the other player's offer. For the union, offers lower than the owners' yield a pay-off lower than agreement, that are settled without appeal to the arbitrator, so that the pay-off is certain. Offers higher than the owners' will result in the arbitrator being called in and the outcome is therefore random. The pay-off function for offers higher than the owners' thus represents the expected utility of the union given its offer, the owners' offer and the behaviour of the arbitrator. Despite the fact that the overall shape of pay-off function depends on the precise form of the utility functions, it is easy to show[14] that the expected pay-offs to disagreement in the neighbourhood of the other player's offer have the general shape shown (that is, both parties will benefit from a small disagreement). The owners' pay-off function is constructed in a similar fashion and is shown in Figure 3b. It is worth stressing that the important feature of these pay-off functions is that they imply that both parties will benefit from a small disagreement. This guarantees that there is a maximum of the pay-off function and that this maximum occurs at a disagreement point when there are no arbitral costs.

In Figure 4, we show the best reply functions associated with these pay-offs. These are derived by taking the set of possible strategies for each player and plotting against each possible strategy the maximum of

FIGURES 3a and 3b
PAYOFF FUNCTIONS FOR CONCILIATION BOARD MODEL, ASSUMING ZERO
COST OR BENEFIT TO CALLING IN THE ARBITRATOR

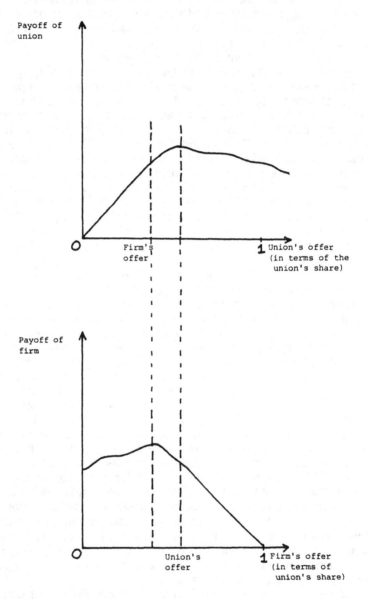

the other player's pay-off function. Consider, for instance, the union's best reply function. If the owners offer the union zero, the union's best reply is to ask for something larger than zero, thus the best reply function has an intercept above the origin on the vertical axis. Because the union's pay-off increases to the right of any agreement point, the best reply lies above the 45° line unless the owners offer the union the whole of the rent. Thus, it is always worthwhile for the union to ask for more than the owners offer. Similarly, the owners' best reply will start from the origin (at which it receives the whole rent) and lie above the 45° line, as shown.[15] It is also reasonable to suppose that these best reply functions are continuous, so that it follows that they will have at least one intersection. A Nash equilibrium in pure strategies exists for this case. Furthermore, because the intersection point must lie above the 45° line, the equilibrium must take the form of disagreement, with a call to the arbitrator being made on each occasion.

FIGURE 4

IF ARBITRATION COSTS ARE ZERO, THE ONLY EQUILIBRIA WILL BE PURE STRATEGY EQUILIBRIA AND ARBITRATOR WILL ALWAYS BE CALLED IN

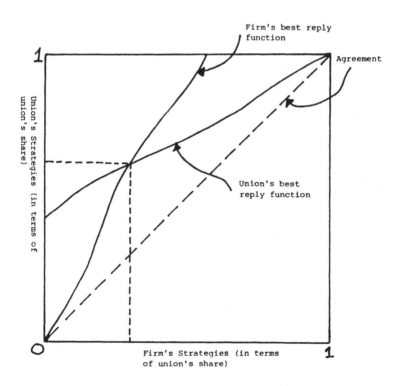

The functions drawn in Figure 3 assume that no cost is incurred when the arbitrator is called. In section II we argued that the possibility of strategic delay yielded a benefit to the owners (cost to the union) when coal prices were rising, and a cost (benefit) when coal prices were falling. Figure 5 shows the effect on the pay-off functions of introducing these costs and benefits when coal prices are rising. It is to introduce a discontinuity at the point of agreement. The owners' function jumps up as their offer to the union gets less generous while the union's function jumps down.

This kind of discontinuity is exactly the kind described in Dasgupta and Maskin in the statement of Theorem 5b.[16] The theorem goes on to state that a game with a discontinuity of this sort always has an equilibrium but does not predict whether it is of the pure or mixed strategy type.[17] In Figure 5 we show the form of the pay-off functions, and in Figure 6 three possible forms of best reply function when this discontinuity is taken into account and when coal prices are rising, so that the owners receive a benefit from strategic delay. For the owners, the form of the best reply function is unaffected by this change. If it was worthwhile for them to call in the arbitrator when no cost was involved, it must still be worthwhile for them to do so if they can gain. The form of the union's best reply is, however, radically changed by the fact that strategic delay is now costly. At the point where the owners offer the union the whole rent, the best reply is still to accept. At the point where the owners offer the union nothing, the best reply depends on whether the cost of arbitration is smaller or greater than the maximum expected pay-off to arbitration. If the cost of arbitration is higher than the maximum expected utility gained by arbitration then the union will be better off accepting the owners' offer. If the cost of arbitration is lower than the maximum expected pay-off to arbitration then the union will be better off calling in the arbitrator. In the latter case, the best reply function must have a discontinuity in it, because as the owners' offer decreases from 1 to 0 there must be some point where the union's best reply switches catastrophically from agreement to disagreement.

It is this possibility of a discontinuity in the best reply function that enables us to predict a qualitative difference in the behaviour of conciliation boards in which strategic delay is permitted by the rules and those in which it is not. If such a discontinuity appears in the best reply function, it is possible that no pure strategy equilibrium will exist and that the only equilibria are mixed strategy ones (Figure 6a). In mixed strategy equilibrium the players will sometimes agree and at other times they will call in the arbitrator.

Other possible configurations are shown in Figures 6b and 6c. In Figure 6b the union's best reply switches twice (it could, of course, conceivably switch more frequently than this). In Figure 6b, the cost of arbitration is so high that the union always agrees.

To end this section we summarise the argument presented above. We claim that a key difference in the constitutions of the conciliation

FIGURES 5a and 5b
PAYOFFS FOR CONCILIATION BOARD MODEL ASSUMING THAT STRATEGIC
DELAY IS POSSIBLE

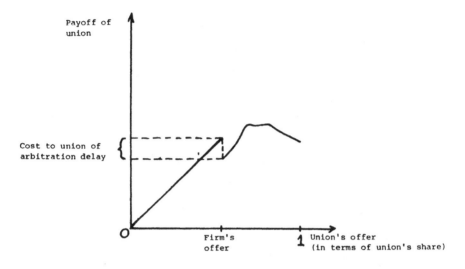

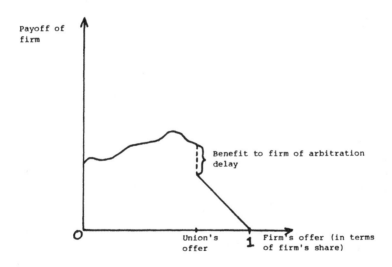

FIGURE 6a

NON-EXISTENCE OF PURE STRATEGY NASH EQUILIBRIUM IN CONCILIATION
BOARD MODEL WITH STRATEGIC DELAY

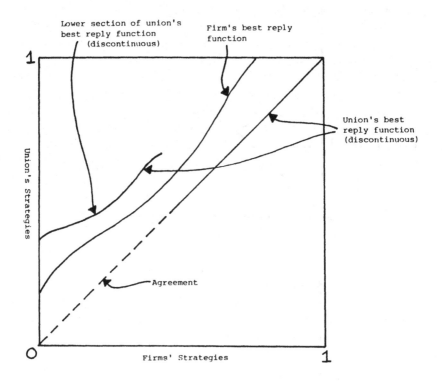

boards is the presence in some but not others of legal opportunities for
strategic delay. Combined with the sliding scale arrangement that
effectively tied the wage rate to the price of coal, these opportunities
meant that it would sometimes be in the interest of one side of the
negotiation to call in the arbitrator, *simply in order to engineer a delay in
the date of the wage rate change.* At the same time, it would be in the
interest of the opposing side to avoid such a delay. It is this tension
between the side wanting delay, and the side wanting immediate
settlement that produces outcomes in which the arbitrator is sometimes
called in and sometimes not. If opportunities for delay are not present
in a constitution, our theory predicts that the arbitrator should always
be called in.

FIGURES 6b and 6c
OTHER POSSIBLE SOLUTIONS WHEN STRATEGIC DELAY IS POSSIBLE. IN VIb
BOTH PURE AND MIXED STRATEGY SOLUTIONS CAN EXIST. IN VIc, THE
ONLY NASH EQUILIBRIUM GIVES THE UNION A SHARE OF ZERO

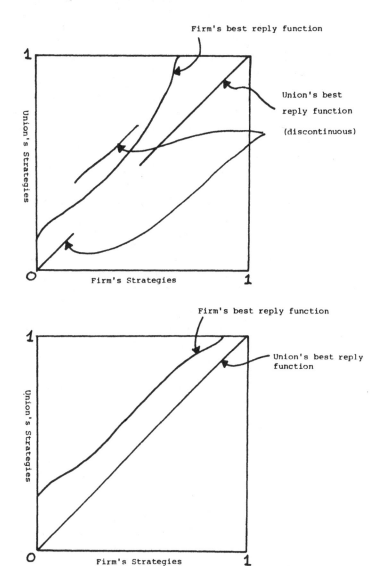

VI

The theoretical structure described above predicts that the South Wales and Northumberland conciliation boards should have had appeals to the arbitrator every quarter. The evidence suggests that although the rate of appeals in these two boards was higher than in the others, it was still substantially less than one. What is wrong with the theory? One assumption that we have made that is not reflected in the conciliation boards' rules is that the strategies lie in a continuous range. As we have seen, the units that were actually used imply that the feasible strategies lay in a discrete set. Incorporating this modification into our diagrams clearly will introduce further discontinuities into the pay-off and best reply functions and will imply some randomisation even when the arbitrator can be called in without cost (or benefit). If this argument is correct, we would expect the spread of offers at the time when the negotiation is referred to the arbitrator to be low in jurisdictions where randomisation is induced only by discreteness of the strategy set. Table 1 indicates that Northumberland has the lowest spread of all the conciliation boards while South Wales is second highest. This is not, of course, a very strong test of our hypothesis, but the fact that spreads and frequency are related at all (the correlation coefficient is -0.75) lends some credence to it.

Are there any other empirical tests suggested by the model presented here? The model predicts that mixed strategies may be used, when the negotiators have best reply functions that do not intersect. Clearly further work is required in order to discover what particular specifications of utility functions and arbitrator behaviour lead to mixed strategy equilibria, and which lead to pure strategy equilibria. Such predictions are in principle testable. Whether the data currently available are sufficient for a convincing test remains to be seen. One important theoretical problem in this field is the calculation of the optimal strategies. In a model whose structure resembles in many respects the model presented here, Osborne and Pitchyk report a failure to calculate exact solutions, and rely on computer generated approximations.[18]

In this paper we have taken issue with Ashley's remark that the observed pattern of appeals to the arbitrator under the conciliation boards is explicable only as the product of personal characteristics of the negotiators. Our alternative explanation, which is based on an analysis of the rules of the boards, is that differential access to strategic delay can be seen as an important factor in determining the frequency of appeals to the arbitrator. The argument is based on a fairly general specification of the problem. In future work we intend to exploit more specific specifications of the pay-offs in an attempt to generate formally testable hypotheses.

University of Hull

NOTES

Thanks are due to Avner Shaked and Simon Vicary for useful conversations, and to Gary Tennant for able research assistance. Earlier versions of this work have been given at seminars at Hull, Queen Mary College (London), Sheffield, London School of Economics and the ESRC Quantitative Economic History Conference at Newcastle upon Tyne (September 1987). The ideas in the article were developed while I was a visitor at the Centre for Labour Economics at LSE, in the spring of 1987. The research underlying the article could not have been done without the cooperation and help of the archivists whose holdings I have used. These are listed in the sources for Table 1. The work would have been impossible, too, without financial support from the ESRC (Contract No.F00232382). My thanks to everyone involved.

1. See J.G. Treble, 'Sliding Scales and Concilation Boards: Risk-sharing in the late 19th Century British Coal Industry', *Oxford Economic Papers*, 39 (1987), pp.679–98.
2. J.G. Treble, 'Perfect Equilibrium Down the Pit: Wage Bargaining Machinery in the late 19th Century British Coal Industry', mimeo (1988), University of Hull.
3. See H.S. Farber, 'An Analysis of Final-Offer Arbitration', *Journal of Conflict Resolution*, Vol.24 (1980), pp.683–705.
4. See V.P. Crawford, 'Arbitration and Conflict Resolution in Labour Management Bargaining', *American Economic Association Papers and Proceedings* (1981), pp.205–10; also, V.P. Crawford, 'A Theory of Disagreement in Bargaining', *Econometrica*, Vol.50 (1982), pp.607–37.
5. For a selection of papers covering a variety of topics in this area see A.E. Roth (ed.), *Game Theoretic Models of Bargaining* (1985).
6. This argument is spelled out in more detail in Treble, 'Perfect Equilibrium'.
7. Here is a simple example: 'Scissors, paper, stone' is a children's game for two players. Each time the game is played, both players hold out their right hand. The players choose either to extend two fingers ('scissors'), to make a fist ('stone'), or hold their hand out flat with the palm down ('paper'). These three alternatives constitute the strategies available to each player. The pay-offs are either 'win', 'lose' or 'draw', and the pay-off function describes how the nine possible combinations of the strategies determine the pay-off for each player. The pay-off function for this game is show in Table 2.

TABLE 1

		Player A's Strategies		
		Scissors	Paper	Stone
P l a y e r	Scissors	Draw, Draw	Lose, Win	Win, Lose
	Paper	Win, Lose	Draw, Draw	Lose, Win
	Stone	Lose, Win	Win, Lose	Draw, Draw
B				

The first entry in each cell is A's pay-off if A plays the column strategy indicated and B plays the row strategy indicated. The second entry is B's pay-off in the same circumstances.

8. For a discussion of rationality and Nash equilibrium, see K. Binmore and P. Dasgupta (eds.), *Economic Organizations as Games* (Oxford, 1986). The reasons for treating the conciliation board negotiations as a non-cooperative game (or contest) are described in Treble, 'Perfect Equilibrium'.
9. See P. Dasgupta and E. Maskin, 'The Existence of Equilibrium in Discontinuous Economic Games, I: Theory', *Review of Economic Studies*, Vol.LIII (1986), pp.1–26.
10. Note that this does not imply the board is useless, since in most arbitral regimes, and certainly in the conciliation boards, the arbitrator's decision is partially determined by the offers of the negotiators.

80 BUSINESS HISTORY: CONCEPTS AND MEASUREMENT

11. See O. Ashenfelter and D.E. Bloom, 'Models of Arbitrator Behaviour: Theory and Evidence', *American Economic Review*, Vol. 74, No.1 (1984), pp.111–24.

12. This could be interpreted as a final-offer arbitrator or as a conventional arbitrator who is limited in his decision by the final offers of the parties. In either case, the arbitrator must be supposed to make decisions according to principles or using data unknown to the bargaining parties. The important assumptions here are: (i) the parties both have the same view of the probabilities involved; (ii) the probabilities used by the arbitrator are not determined by the offers. Note that this formulation allows arbitral bias. This is captured by setting the probability used by the arbitrator to a value different from half.

13. In order to draw Figure 3, we have to make some assumption about what the outcome will be if the union's claim is lower than the owner's offer. In order to ensure that such a situation will never arise as an outcome of rational play, we need to specify that the pay-off to such strategy pairs is always less for both parties than the pay-off to agreement. One way of doing this is to suppose that in such cases the union receives its claim and the owners receive their offer. This assumption is built into Figure 3.

14. The proof can be found in Treble, 'Perfect Equilibrium'. It relies on the assumption that the utility functions and the density of the arbitrator's decision are all differentiable, but is otherwise general.

15. The best reply line can never cross the 45° line because this would mean one party claiming from the other less for itself than the other is prepared to give.

16. See Dasgupta and Maskin, 'Existence of Equilibrium'.

17. See also L. Simon, 'Games with Discontinuous Payoffs', *Review of Economic Studies*, Vol.LIV, No.4 (1987), pp.569–98.

18. M. Osborne and C. Pitchyk, 'Equilibrium in Hotelling's Model of Spatial Competition', *Econometrica*, Vol.55 (4) (1987), pp.911–22.

COMPETITION, CO-OPERATION AND NATIONALISATION IN THE NINETEENTH CENTURY TELEGRAPH SYSTEM

By JAMES FOREMAN-PECK

Victorians did not generally regard nationalisation favourably. If both free market behaviour and armslength regulation proved unsatisfactory, the regulation of industries such as gas and water might be internalised by municipal ownership so that local interests were able to oversee local services.[1] When the performance of national services was called into question, as it was with the railway network, increasingly detailed armslength regulation was preferred, albeit with less than perfect results.[2] True, the national postal network remained state owned, but special characteristics, in particular the lack of capital employed, together with the Rowland Hill reforms, accounted for the high prestige of this nationalised industry by the 1860s.[3]

The early telecommunications network is a curious exception in Victorian industrial policy. Unusually by European standards, the United Kingdom began with a private system which was nationalised after 24 years because of public concern about the service. Nationalisation was supported by most newspapers, which resented the telegraph companies' monopoly of the news, and by Chambers of Commerce which felt the service was too expensive, inaccurate and insufficiently widespread geographically. The Post Office saw an opportunity to remedy this last defect by employing existing sub-post offices as telegraph stations in a Post Office-owned system.[4]

Under Acts of 1868 and 1869, nationalisation did indeed spread telegraph service and greatly increased the use of the system, but soon the network was running at a loss. Investigation by a Treasury committee made no impression upon the growing deficit.[5]

In the light of the privatisation policies of the 1980s, these facts themselves are striking, but so too are the issues they raise for British industrial history. Apparently neither the privately owned nor the nationalised industry were especially satisfactory organisational forms for the nineteenth-century telegraph. In the following two sections, first, the expansion of the private industry, and then the growth of the Post Office system are described with a view to identifying the salient features of telegraph development which caused public dissatisfaction. The models which can explain and evaluate the behaviour of the industry in the two stages are discussed in the third section. The fourth section then presents evidence for and against these models so that some judgement can be reached as to the strengths and weaknesses of the two forms and how they might have been improved.

I

The Process of Competition and Co-operation

Whereas the American industry by the late 1860s came to be dominated by one firm, Western Union, British market concentration declined almost continually throughout the private enterprise period. The Herfindhal index of British telegraph concentration fell from 1 in 1849 to 0.56 in 1855, reaching a nadir of 0.27 in 1861, rising again to 0.47 in 1865 and ending in 1868 at 0.41.[6] The strategy of the incumbent British firm, the Electric and International Telegraph Company (the 'Electric' or EITC) was to establish a profitable 'modus vivendi' with other firms in the industry, even if that meant losing market share. By contrast, Western Union absorbed and rationalised rival enterprises. The greater role of mergers and concentration in American industrial organisation is often attributed to the 1890 Sherman Act. Since the legislation had not then been passed, it cannot explain the divergent courses of telegraph concentration in the two countries before 1868.

In response to new entry, the Electric's tariff reductions in 1852, 1854, 1862 and 1864–65 were significant sources of sales growth for the company itself and for the industry (Table 1). The EITC's profitability suffered most with the tariff reductions of 1854. Thereafter price stability appears to have been maintained until the entry of the United Kingdom Telegraph Co. (UKTC). (Although the London and District made inroads into the EITC's apparent market share, in fact the service offered was probably not directly competitive). After an agreement had been reached with the entrants in 1856, the Electric doubled the London–Birmingham tariff and increased the rates on the Manchester–Liverpool and Manchester–Leeds routes by 50 per cent.[7] The Electric reduced the number of stations by one-fifth between 1850–52 and then almost doubled the number of offices open to the public in the following two years (Table 1). 1859 saw a reduction in the number of offices but the advent of the UKTC caused a massive expansion in 1861; again offices open to the public nearly doubled in two years. Entry of the UKTC with a uniform one shilling tariff was met by Electric tariff cuts at nearly 200 places, but only where the Electric faced competition.

The established companies owned the rights of way for telegraph lines along railway routes yet this was not an insurmountable entry barrier. The UKTC put up lines instead alongside public roads, a policy which the incumbent firms bitterly resisted by legal proceedings. 'Men therefore were employed to traverse the roads, suggesting opposition and making the grossest misrepresentations; counsel's opinion of an adverse character were obtained and circulated, suggesting how this company's poles should be cut down'.[8] Profitability of the Electric reached a trough in 1862, as the company's price cut restored most of

TABLE 1

THE ELECTRIC TELEGRAPH COMPANY IN THE BRITISH MARKET 1849–1868

Year	Event	% Growth of EITC paid Public Messages	EITC Average Tariff (Revenue per Message)	EITC % Market Share	EITC Stations	EITC Profit to Turnover Ratio
1849	ETC pays first dividend 30th June. The rival British Electric Telegraph Co. (BETC) formed and incorporated by an act of July 1850, opposed by the ETC.	n.a.	n.a.	100	n.a.	
1850	ETC's wires on only 2215 miles of railway out of 7231. 64734 messages sent. In the US over 12,000 miles of telegraph and 20 telegraph cos.	n.a.	.50	n.a.	257	
1851	English and Irish Magnetic Telegraph Co. (EIM) incorporated. Numbers of messages transmitted accelerate. 20 words less than 100 mls, 2/6, over 100 mls, 5/-.	53	.50	n.a.	224	.38
1852		113	.32	n.a.	207	.35
1853	Rates further reduced	16	.42	n.a.	338	.30
1854		133	.21	n.a.	420	.25
1855	ETC and International Telegraph Co. merged to create the EITC. Permitted by the Electric Telegraph Act which placed a 10% dividend limit. Within London 1/-, up to 50 mls, 1/6, up to 100 mls 2/-.	25	.20	70	404	.30
1856	BETC and EIM amalgamate to form 'The Magnetic' under the Joint Stock Companies Act of 1856.	7	.21	68	423	.33
1857		10	.21	68	460	.33
1858		3	.20	66	517	.32
1859	London and District Telegraph Company formed. Offers service at 4d for 10 words, 6d for 15 words.	18	.20	63	428	.34
1860	UK Telegraph Company formed with a uniform one shilling rate.	9	.19	60	476	.32
1861	Ricardo, former director of Electric Telegraph C., writes memo advocating nationalisation.	7	.19	45	772	.33
1862	London and South of Ireland Telegraph Co. formed.	28	.14	57	900	.30
1863	Telegraph Act restricts the sale of telegraph companies without the consent of the Board of Trade.	19	.14	56	1022	.35
1864		29	.11	50	1022	.36
1865	The three companies introduce a new tariff as the UK abandons the one shilling rate. National Assoc. of Chambers of Commerce Committee report on poor telegraph service.	26	.11	47	1180	.40
1866	Snow brings down many miles of line.	6	.11	n.a.	1249	.39
1867		6	.10	n.a.	1249	.39
1868	Act authorising state purchase of telegraph Companies.	12	n.a.	57	n.a.	.44

the market share lost in 1861. Rapid sales growth and an expansion of offices was however insufficient to prevent a reversal of the gain over the following three years. The company lost money on the one shilling tariff on the London to Liverpool and London to Manchester routes and was obliged to put up more wires to cope with the traffic generated.[9] However, the Electric possessed the resources to survive the price war and therefore was able ultimately to dictate peace terms. In September 1864 the conditions for ending the tariff war were that the UKTC was to make no further extensions for two years in return for the EIT maintaining prices.[10] Almost one year later, in June 1865, the UKTC proposed that the rate for inland messages be increased for up to 100 miles, to 1s., up to 200 miles to 1s.6d. and over 200 miles, to 2s. The proposal was accepted on the condition that the UKTC publicly announce in each town where they had a station that the uniform one shilling rate had proved a failure.

The price agreement of 1865 ushered in a period of slower sales growth, greater market share and profitability rising to unprecedented levels. A portion of the greater profitability is attributable to the reduction of maintenance expenditure and the ending of expansion after 1866, when the nationalisation debate began. Investment in expansion of the system was typically charged to current expenditure. The response to the first entry was then price cuts and reduction of offices and to all subsequent new entrants a price cut and an expansion of offices. In all cases the ultimate aim of the tactic was to form a cartel which fixed prices.

British management only seem to have appreciated the possibilities of merger, rather than a cartel, as a result of a visit by Western Union's Cyrus Field in 1864. The secretary to the Electric, Weaver, was impressed by Field's account of combining American telegraph companies to maintain profit rates and yet at the same time offering cheap tariffs.[11] Weaver was particularly interested in the techniques for amalgamations; how prices were agreed for shares (such as those of some of his rivals) trading at a 50 per cent discount, and whether amalgamated companies worked as an integrated system or maintained all their old offices. Ultimately, in response to the nationalisation threat, the principal British companies did try to rationalise after a fashion. In December 1867 they held a special meeting about the transfer of the telegraphs to the state and discussed a traffic working agreement between the three companies.[12] Before then, working arrangements had been restricted to companies whose interests were clearly complementary. The British Electric Telegraph Co., incorporated in 1850, early boasted a connection with the Submarine Telegraph Co.[13] The successor Magnetic Telegraph Co. reached an agreement with the London and District in 1859. Very differently, the dominant firm, the Electric, seems to have found problems achieving cooperative working, in contrast to cooperative pricing, with almost anybody, even the Submarine. Difficulties between these two companies were the subject of unsuccessful negotiations in 1856, 1858 and 1860. On the last occasion the Electric was urging the Submarine to maintain charges for continental messages while in Paris asking for a concession on another line at a greatly reduced tariff.[14] Aggression towards rivals combined with timidity where technological advances were concerned. The Electric's chairman, Grimston, declined to support the cause of Atlantic telegraphy in 1866 by buying shares, on the grounds that they were 'speculative'.[15] And this despite the recognition of the key importance for business of international connections. Perhaps the Electric's only successful co-operation in working was the agreement with the Universal Private Telegraph Co. which supplied private line services and therefore did not compete in public traffic. A more co-operative or creative dominant firm could have constructed a rather different industry.

II

Nationalisation

Under the companies in 1868 there were 2,155 public telegraph offices and 1226 railway offices which the public might use. By 1872, Post Office telegraph stations totalled 3,444.[16] Railway offices were a good deal more abundant in the mid-1870s as well but thereafter their numbers declined until the end of the decade. The volume of telegraph traffic leaped upwards. In the year ending March 1871, 9.8 million messages were sent, compared with 6.4 million in the calendar year 1868. During the financial year 1872, traffic volume was almost twice the 1868 total (Table 2). Both the number of instruments and employment had approximately doubled between the transfer and August 1870. Traffic was responding not merely to the reduction of long distance tariffs to the uniform one shilling rate but to more free porterage for messages, more free words for names and addresses on the telegrams and a more convenient arrangements of offices.

Transfer of telegraphs to the state proved far more expensive than had been expected. Economies of scale and scope were not realised sufficiently to counter other increased costs such as porterage. Negotiations with the railways to buy out their rights proved a lengthy and expensive business. Assimilation of the workforce to civil service pay and conditions was another stimulus to costs. Telegraph employees were not altogether happy with the new arrangement, obtaining back-dated pay awards in 1872 after a strike, and showing higher propensity to join a union than under the companies.[17] Hours of work were reduced from ten or twelve to eight and a supervisory class was introduced. In the Engineering division, 248 established officers in 1875 supervised 350 established linesmen and mechanics. Rapid expansion after the transfer accounted for the inflated numbers of the supervisory class but did not justify their continuing employment. Variation in

TABLE 2

THE TELEGRAPH SERVICE UNDER THE POST OFFICE: FISCAL YEARS 1871–1894

	Telegraph Messages Forwarded ('000)	Working Expenses (£000)
1871	9850	394
1872	12474	592
1873	15536	875
1874	17821	968
1875	19253	1077
1876	20978	1031
1877	21726	1124
1878	22172	1164
1879	24460	1089
1880	26547	1111
1881	29412	1242
1882	31346	1366
1883	32092	1504
1884	32843	1709
1885	33278	1731
1886	39146	1733
1887	50244	1940
1888	55183	1928
1889	59559	1969
1890	64103	2180
1891	68622	2265
1982	72154	2507
1893	72303	2567
1894	73300	2641

Note: Minor changes in coverage are included in these series.
Sources: Postmaster General's Reports and Annual Abstracts of Statistics.

workforces between offices and over time indicated overmanning in some places. Edinburgh central office sent 50,000 more messages than Dublin, yet cost £7,092 less. Between 1872 and 1873 Edinburgh increased the volume of messages sent by 50 per cent with no increase in clerks. Dublin transmitted almost half as many telegrams again in 1876 as in 1872, yet managed to reduce the number of clerks employed from 401 to 286.[18]

Ten years after the transfer of the telegraphs to the state, the Postmaster-General boasted of the doubling of the number of telegraph offices and an approximately fourfold expansion of messages sent and instruments in use. Employment had increased less than proportionately with messages; telegraphists roughly doubled their numbers and messengers tripled.[19] These figures did appear to vindicate earlier claims that there were economies of scale, of scope or of integration.

In 1883 the government acquiesced in a House of Commons resolution that the charge for a telegram be reduced to 6d. Introduced in October 1885, the tariff cut expanded messages from 33 million in 1884/85 to 50 million in 1886/87. Until the implementation of this tariff, revenue had exceeded expenditure to meet at least some of the interest on the stock created for the acquisition of the telegraphs. Pay awards in August 1881 and in July 1890 pushed the telegraphs further in the red.[20] In this last round, telegraphist wages were raised to a level about 20 per cent above that of 1875. Low grade engineering staff achieved very little until the end of the 1890s but high grade engineers were receiving 65 per cent more than their mid-1870s pay by the early 1890s.[21]

The 1875 Treasury Committee had commented that the very low press tariff was a source of loss to the service yet the power of the press was such that no action was taken before the outbreak of the First World War, even when it had been established that the concession was costing around £200,000 a year.[22] Free railway messages negotiated under the 1868 Act were also a source of loss for the telegraph service. Between 1871 and 1890 the volume of this traffic in England and Wales increased more than twelvefold to just over 1.2 million. Unlike the press, the railways were persuaded to accept a curtailment of their 1868 privileges in the form of an upper limit on the number of words and messages that they were permitted without charge.

Under state as under private ownership, the industry maintained price stability for long periods, with an occasional concession to customers. In contrast to the private industry, the principal goal of the state telegraph service was not earning profits but extending the service, subsidised by the post. The pressure to do so, operating through Parliament, was far stronger than for the private industry. Among the few countervailing forces was the greater tendency for wage costs to rise.

III

Models

Alternating price competition and cooperation expanded output from just under 65,000 public messages (excluding railway and press telegrams) in 1850 to about 100 times than number when the nationalisation Act was passed in 1868. Despite similar technology, over the period British industrial concentration declined, whereas in the United States it rose. A number of contemporaries thought that the technical characteristics of the the telegraph were such that one firm *could* supply services more cheaply than two or more (which is not to say that any one firm *would*); there were economies of scale or scope or both.[23] Possibly the fixed costs of the industry, such as the poles or trenches which carried the wire, or the telegraph office, were sufficient to lower the average costs of a firm as it grew bigger, by spreading the overheads over a larger volume of output. The biggest firm could therefore temporarily charge prices that new entrants to the industry were unable to match in the long run and thereby ultimately insist on price leadership, a cartel or a monopoly.

Alternatively or in addition, the costs of sending a telegram along one route may have been reduced by the possession of a network that supplied a number of related routes, again because of the sharing of fixed costs. In this case working arrangements between companies could in principle equalise the unit costs of a multiple firm industry with those of a monopoly. In so far as this technical feature was important, the transactions costs of agreeing working arrangements relative to the private benefits appear to have been too high for the British industry. Neither price competition nor price cooperation emerge as ideal in this instance, since they entail wasteful duplication of plant.

If larger telegraph companies were more efficient, then a puzzle remains as to how other, smaller, firms entered the industry and survived. Darwinistic 'survivor' arguments suggest that advantages of scale or the scope of operations in an industry is revealed by increases in market shares of larger firms or of those with a wider spread of activities or routes.[24] An extreme formulation is that the size and scope configuration of firms at any point in time demonstrates the underlying cost structure of the industry at that date.[25] Contrary to these hypotheses, British concentration may have fallen despite economies of scale and scope through a failure to minimise costs, a deterioration in the quality of entrepreneurship or management. Lapses from best practice by the incumbent firm provide opportunities for entrants who offer a stimulus to efficiency.

A second type of explanation appeals to pricing policy rather than to costs. Either entry was allowed by high profit margins and the willingness of entrant firms to accept lower profitability, or the technical nature and market of the industry did not permit the dominant firm to charge entry-deterring prices. In the first case, the Electric preferred short term monopoly pricing and lower future profits after entry because of a high discount rate relative to Western Union's. In the second, once entry had taken place, a competitive equilibrium did not exist and therefore some form of cooperation had to be found; a cartel, regulation or a merger.[26] In contrast to the later telephone, pricing for access to, rather than use of, the telegraph network was difficult. The telegraph office was a type of public good. It was available to all who lived in the neighbourhood even though only regular users paid. Moreover, senders of telegrams could not easily be charged marginal cost prices since total revenues were unlikely to cover the costs of the offices. With price competition from new entrants, prices were likely to be forced down to marginal costs.[27] For the whole market then competition would ultimately prove unsustainable, and either a monopoly, or a cartel would emerge.

Another form of competition, in which firms choose their output rates, can lead to an equilibrium in which prices are higher and costs are covered, but there are too many firms in the industry for full advantage to be taken of economies of scale.[28] A similar phenomenon can occur in the spatial dimension. Firms locate offices to steal each others' business so that they cluster in town centres and leave outlying regions unserved.[29]

These price and output non-cooperative equilibria are not necessarily mutually exclusive. Output decisions can be regarded as long-term investment plans, which will be influenced by those of competitors. Short-term price decisions can diverge from the planned long-run prices if entry takes place and market shares and profitability are to be maintained.

Economies of scale or scope may have been barriers to entry, but at least they were not insurmountable in contrast to the Act of 1869. Consequently before the transfer to the state the threat of entry may have encouraged a larger network of offices as a deterrent to entrants even though those offices in outlying regions were perhaps making no contribution to the overheads of the central organisation of the firm. In the face of entry the incumbents increased output. It was therefore rational to maintain some unused capacity before entry to facilitate the output reaction and to ensure prospective entrants knew how the incumbent would react.[30] A spread of facilities to outlying regions may therefore have been as extensive as was feasible, given the available economies of scope.

In the presence of economies of scale and scope the market cannot always be relied upon to select an optimum industry organisation. Some form of political intervention may be required as in 1868 and 1869. That is not to assert that political restructuring will not typically impose alternative inefficiencies. There is an institutional spectrum of possible industry organisations that will generate a spectrum of outcomes for a range of variables. As far as the telegraph industry is concerned that spectrum includes at a minimum:

(1) a profit-maximising privately owned monopolist,
(2) a cartel,
(3) a competitive industry with firms choosing output,
(4) a competitive industry with firms choosing price,
(5) a regulated industry with working arrangements enforced and some form of protection for the consumer against monopolistic exploitation,
(6) a nationalised industry subject to manipulation by consumer and producer groups,
(7) a social welfare maximising state owned or regulated industry.

On theoretical grounds, a private monopoly was likely to be able and willing to offer lower prices and costs than a cartel which exercised the same market power but did not attain the economies of scale or scope of the monopoly. On that reckoning the British pattern before 1870 was the worst of both worlds. Nationalisation at least created an integrated monopoly. The state industry may also have avoided exploitation as well. On the other hand state ownership and legal entry barriers may have removed pressures for the internal efficiency of the organisation.

Costs may have risen so that price exploitation would have occurred, except that the Post Office telegraph received subsidies, so that other customers (postal users) instead were unfairly treated.

The most pertinent comparison for the purposes of the present study is between a nationalised industry and some combination of types (2), (3) and (4). During the nationalisation debate, Belgium and Switzerland were often held up as countries with telegraph administrations of the type to which the United Kingdom should aspire. Empirical comparison must be brought in because, as the above discussion has shown, for the most part, the models indicate possibilities rather than clearly determined behavioural outcomes.

IV

Analysis

As a means of discriminating between different models of the industry, first data on 'business stealing' through excessive entry to an industry or market, or 'clustering', under the private industry, and integration or utilisation of economies of scope under the state, is assembled. Such material might indicate the presence or absence of the phenomenon but cannot indicate how important it is. The two principal pieces of evidence therefore are a comparison of time series cost functions for the state and privately owned industries and a systematic international comparison of telegrams sent, which reflects international cost function and demand differences.

Tables 3 and 4 present some evidence of excessive entry into the private British industry of 1868. The number of messages per office was small compared to most other systems. That might be interpreted as an indication that competition was successful in spreading telegraph facilities into outlying regions where demand was less strong, were it not that total telegrams sent per head were also quite low by international standards. Low labour productivity supports the judgement that the industry was not behaving in an ideal fashion.

A caveat is that the output measure in this comparison fails to take into account variations in the quality of service between national systems. Speed of delivery and accuracy were vital attributes in determining the advantage of the telegram over the post for certain types of message. Although the Post Office complaints of the two hour or more waiting time for its own telegrams were part of the evidence accumulated to support nationalisation, in international terms the British system, both before and after the transfer to the state, was almost certainly above average, judged by these criteria. The Director-General of the Belgian Telegraphs pointed out that the low half franc tariff had been forced upon Belgium by the terms of the 1865 Convention.[31] A great number of telegrams were sent but without either speed or accuracy; the half franc messages were forwarded by post. If speed

TABLE 3
NATIONAL TELEGRAPH SYSTEMS AND INCOME c.1868

	Telegraph Messages Per Head	National Product Per Head 1870	Telegraph Wires Per Line	Telegrams ('000) per Office	Telegrams ('000) per Mile of Line	Telegrams ('000) per Mile of Wire
United Kingdom (1868)	0.203	904	4.742	1.904	0.381	0.080
United States (Western Union) (1868)	0.166	791	1.945	1.990	0.128	0.065
France (1869)	0.148	567	2.826	1.924	0.209	0.073
Belgium (1869)	0.339	738	3.177	3.934	0.659	0.207
Switzerland * (1868)	0.432	589	2.163	2.512	0.406	0.187
Holland * (1868)	0.418	591	2.784	18.024	1.222	0.438
Italy (1870)	0.082	467	2.882	1.761	0.198	0.068
Austria (1870)	0.166	446	3.188	2.800	0.294	0.092
Hungary (1870)	0.096	345	2.738	3.057	0.248	0.090
Spain (1868)	0.047	391	2.017	6.434	0.175	0.086
Germany (1868)	0.146	579	3.292	3.099	0.407	0.123
Denmark (1870)	0.288	563	2.598	6.853	0.422	0.162
Sweden (1868)	0.121	351	1.967	5.409	0.127	0.064
Norway (1870)	0.257	441	1.454	4.667	0.126	0.087
Russia (1868)	0.027	252	1.906	3.585	0.082	0.042

Notes: Columns 2–6 refer to 1869 for Switzerland, 1867 for Germany, 1866 for Sweden, 1860 for Spain.
* = State system only.

Sources: N.F.R. Crafts, 'Gross National Product in Europe 1870–1910: Some New Estimates', *Exploration in Economic History*, xx (1983), pp.387–401. UK *Abstract of Statistics for Foreign Countries*; M.J. Brown, *Report on the Working of the French, Belgian and Swiss Telegraphic Systems* (HMSO 1870), Post Office Archivem Post 83/66; and Anon., *Report on Government Telegraphy in the Netherlands*, (1871) Post 83/67.

TABLE 4

TELEGRAPH NETWORK LABOUR PRODUCTIVITY c.1868

		Messages Sent (000)	Employment	Messages per employee
United Kingdom	(1868)	6438	5339	1206
France	(1869)	5346	3709	1441
Belgium	(1869)	1723	982	1754
Switzerland	(1869)	1369	607	2255
Italy	(1870)	2189	2676	818
Germany (excluding Wurtemburg and Bavaria)	(1867)	4380	2934	1493
Russia	(1868)	2029	3453	587
Sweden	(1866)	419	375	1117
Denmark	(1870)	514	191	2691

Sources: UK *Statistical Abstract for Foreign Countries*; M.J. Brown, Post 83/66, op. cit.; Anon., Post 83/67, op. cit.

was required, a tariff three times that rate was charged and for really urgent telegrams, the fee was two francs. In view of the central role played by the Belgian service in the case of nationalisation of the British telegraph system, this qualification is of considerable importance. It should be noted, however, that the companies in the United Kingdom charged porterage for messages sent to destinations further than half a mile from the telegraph office.

Possibly the relatively low number of messages per employee in the United Kingdom was a consequence of the need to maintain capacity to send messages quickly even during the busy hours (10 a.m. to 1 p.m). A similar argument cannot be applied to the messages to offices ratio though. Inspection of the pattern of telegraph offices in the large towns at the time of the transfer to the State does not offer support for an efficient private industry. Typically, large areas were unserved and offices of rival companies were grouped together. In Edinburgh the majority of the nine stations were in two clusters at Leith and Princes Street/Hanover Street. Glasgow, with 13 stations was better served but again they fell into two groups and four of the offices belonged to the private line UPTC.[32] A simple index of spatial dispersion sums the ratio (the distance of each office to the nearest office)/(the distance of each office from the nearest office of the same company). The index tends to zero as competitive clustering increases. For Glasgow the index was 0.5 and for Edinburgh 0.39.

With the Post Office takeover there were clear examples of system integration. The Magnetic owned a circuit from Bristol through Gloucester to Birmingham and London. The UKTC owned a virtually useless Gloucester to Uxbridge circuit. The Post Office joined the lines at Gloucester and extended the circuit from Uxbridge to London. In so doing three high traffic routes were created; London–Birmingham, London–Bristol and Bristol–Gloucester, with three intermediate stations.[33] By introducing a switch into the central telegraph office in London, the Post Office established direct connection with a greater number of branch offices, so reducing delivery time. Another device to the same end was the extension of the city pneumatic tube delivery systems, investment in which became more desirable with a unitary organisation.[34]

A Comparison of Cost Functions

Such improvements will have reduced the costs of supplying a given volume of industry services but in the narrative section of this article there were suggestions that the nationalised industry brought higher costs in other respects which might have more than offset increased utilisation of economies of scope. In order to test that proposition a simple cost comparison between the EITC and the Post Office telegraph is presented. Ideally a comparison with the entire private industry would be undertaken. Lack of data precludes that option and the test is therefore biased against the state regime. The output of the dominant firm is likely to have been produced at lower costs than that of the smaller firms in the industry that were less profitable.

Formulations of cost functions must take into consideration the tendency for both the companies and the Post Office to charge investment in the extension of the telegraph system to current costs. A second property the functions should possess is an allowance for the pace of expansion, and changes in factor prices, upon costs, as the account of the growth of the Post Office system indicated. Maintenance outlays were conventionally included in current costs even though the traffic which had imposed the necessity for that expenditure had been carried in the past. The basic function is assumed to be:

$$C = a_0 + a_1Q + a_2W + a_3T$$

where C is working cost as conventionally defined, Q is messages sent, W is a factor price index, T is a measure of technical progress and a_i are parameters, a_4, a_1, $a_2 > 0$, $a_3 < 0$. Expansion and adjustments costs are

$$EC = a_4 (Q - Q_{-1}) + a_5 (W - W_{-1})$$

where the subscript -1 indicates a one period lag and a_4, $a_5 > 0$. Some portion of current maintenance expenditures will have been incurred because of traffic and traffic growth in earlier periods. Measured costs TC, will therefore include the term $a_6 TC_{-1}$ ($a_6 > 0$) to reflect maintenance costs.

$$TC = a_0 + a_1Q + a_2W + a_3T + a_4(Q-Q_{-1}) + a_5(W-W_{-1}) + a_6TC_{-1}$$

To improve the parameter estimates, the first difference (Δ) of measured working costs is the dependent variable in the first order error correction estimating equation.

$$\Delta TC = a_0 + (a_1 + a_4)\Delta Q + (a_2 + a_5)\Delta W + a_1 Q_{-1} + a_2 W_{-1} + a_3 T + (a_6 - 1)TC_{-1}$$

Telegraph organisations had to respond to the demand for telegrams at their offices and that determined their costs. Causation did not also run from costs to messages and therefore OLS estimation is appropriate. The principal difficulty in obtaining data for the variables of the estimating equation arises for the factor price and technology variables. For technology the best that can be done is a time trend. For factor prices, under the EITC only a general wholesale price index is available, but for the Post Office, wage indices could be obtained.[35] EITC working costs and messages are summarised by Price Williams and for the Post Office these variables are recorded in the Postmaster-General's Reports and the Annual Abstracts of Statistics.[36]

The equations below are estimated in logarithms and with T excluded since it contributed nothing to the explanation of the change in costs. All variables in the EITC equation have the expected signs. The coefficients on lagged telegrams and costs imply very strong increasing returns to scale. A one per cent increase in messages sent raised costs by only 0.33 per cent. This result includes the effects of technical progress on costs, as well as output. The Post Office equation is less satisfactory, with the lagged price index showing the wrong sign. The long-run scale coefficient, at 0.47, is almost half as high again as the EITC's. That may be because of a slower intrinsic rate of technical progress in the later stages of telegraph development, but it does not bear out grandiose claims for the superiority of a unitary state organisation over a private firm. An F test on the two equations shows that their parameters when taken together are significantly different from each other (SSR for the pooled equation is 0.2558). Not surprisingly, the equations allow a rejection of the hypothesis that the EITC costs behaved similarly to the Post Office's.

More interesting is the Post Office equation with the wage index replacing the wholesale price index. The explanatory power of the equation is improved and all the coefficients are statistically significant with the correct signs. The long run scale coefficient remains virtually the same (0.48) and the estimate of the long run wage elasticity is greater than one. This last probably reflects the tendency for wage awards to be backdated. Although how an EITC equation with a wage index would compare cannot be known, the two Post Office equations are consistent with a change in the employment and wage bargaining regime under the Post Office that the qualitative sources indicate. Equally it is not impossible that the later nineteenth-century evolution of the national labour market would have altered EITC cost behaviour in the absence of a state takeover. Yet Weaver's response in 1866 to circulars promoting the Telegraph Clerks' Association, that no one associated should find employment in any telegraph company in Great

TABLE 5

EITC AND POST OFFICE TELEGRAPH COST FUNCTIONS (DEPENDENT
VARIABLE, CHANGE IN WORKING COSTS)

	(1) EITC 1851-1868 (Calendar years)	(2) PO 1871-1894 (Fiscal years)	(3) PO 1871-1894 (Fiscal years)
Const.	.6544	2.0478	-2.7630
	(.7474)	(.7500)	(2.265)
Δ Q	.0682	.1984	.3799
	(1.0507)	(.6379)	(2.3390)
Δ P	.8862	.4078	
	(3.4547)	(1.3469)	
Q-1	.1436	.1972	.3309
	(2.9970)	(1.2788)	(4.7911)
P-1	.1049	-.2086	
	(.4946)	(.5655)	
TC-1	-.4317	-.4223	-.6869
	(4.2710)	(4.2506)	(5.9424)
Δ W			.8579
			(3.0293)
W-1			.9333
			(2.728)
R²	.8942	.6706	.7202
DW	1.89	1.36	1.51
SSR	.02116	.07174	.0809

Notes: All variables in logs. White heteroscedastic consistent t statistics in parentheses. P and W are respectively the wholesale price index and the Routh wage index.

Britain, was not likely to encourage unionisation as much as the more accommodating Post Office approach.[37] The conclusion that Post Office telegraph costs were greater than the EITC's would have been, is not proved, but seems highly likely.

An International Comparison of Telegraph Use

The Post Office need not have behaved in the way it did, nor need the private industry. Alternative models of organisation and behaviour were available on the continent. An international comparison of telegraph usage at the time the nationalisation Act was passed can provide further insights into what was possible. In such a comparison competitive duplication of facilities is taken into account which it is not in the cost function comparison. The approach followed is described more formally elsewhere.[38] The basic principle is to estimate a reduced form relationship which includes both demand and cost influences. The method has the advantage of eliminating the need to compare international price or cost structures for telegrams of different lengths or being sent different distances, by substituting these terms out.

Richer people are likely to require to communicate more, both because household demand is responsive to income and because communication-intensive services become more important with economic development. For a given level of efficiency of a telegraph network, higher income countries will therefore have sent more telegrams, and at similar income levels, countries with more efficient telegraph networks would have also sent more messages. Table 6 shows that despite the highest income per head of the sample, the United Kingdom did not use the telegraph most intensively. Other factors influenced demand and supply apart from income but the joint impact of these cannot be inferred easily from the table. A regression model of the form:

$$Q/PP = b_0 + b_1Y + b_2P + b_3A + b_4S$$

(where Q/PP is telegrams sent per head of population, Y is national product, A is area of the country and S is the subsidy or profit per message) is therefore estimated.[39] Larger countries almost certainly had a longer average haul of messages, which would have been more expensive; a negative coefficient on the area variable is predicted. Systems serving larger populations for given areas and incomes required more infrastructure which must have raised costs; a negative effect on messages sent is expected. A subsidy, which does not lead to offsetting reductions in efficiency, may be anticipated to increase telegraph use. The subsidy was measured by the ratio of revenue to expenditure for each national system; the higher the subsidy the lower the ratio of income to spending. Since the subsidy coefficient had the incorrect sign and was statistically significant (suggesting subsidies did cause offsetting inefficiency), the variable is not included in the reported equations.

Equation (1) in Table 6 is estimated from the countries with state systems and then predicts telegrams sent per head on the assumption that the same relationship held for the United States (the only other major private enterprise system) and the United Kingdom. The F statistic tests for structural change between the samples including and excluding these two countries.

Equation (2) is estimated including the US in the sample. Measurement errors for telegrams per head are a source of the error term on which the regression model depends and do not bias the parameter estimates. Errors in the measurement of national product are likely to be larger and, because they cannot be included in the error term of the OLS model, they can bias all the coefficients. To correct for this possibility, rail miles was used as an instrumental variable for national product in equation (3). The coefficients and the prediction change little.

In all cases the equations predict a higher telegraph penetration for Britain than was actually attained in 1868. On the other hand in no case can the hypothesis that (the American and) the British system behaved similarly to those of other countries be rejected. Equation (1) indicates that the two free enterprise systems were performing worse than predicted from the state network sample. In the American case, both the after-effects of the Civil War and the exclusion of non-Western Union networks suggest true US performance may have been close to

TABLE 6

REGRESSION ANALYSIS OF TELEGRAPH USE ACROSS NATIONS c.1868
(DEPENDENT VARIABLE, MESSAGES PER HEAD OF POPULATION)

	Estimation Method	Constant	National Product	Population	Area	$\bar{R}^2$	SSR	Prediction US	Prediction UK	F-Test for structural change
(1)	OLS	-8.50 [5.36]	1.63 [9.42]	-1.95 [10.94]	-.05 [-.64]	.842	1.0046	.20	.30	.16
(2)	OLS	-7.88 [9.18]	1.56 [10.73]	-1.87 [-12.84]	-.07 [-1.98]	.845	1.0043	.170	.284	.73
(3)	IV	-7.43 [7.72]	1.49 [9.49]	-1.80 [.16]	-.07 [2.08]	-	1.0099	.164	.272	.70
				Actual ··············				.17 (Western Union Only)	.20	

Notes: Equation (1) excludes both the US and the UK, equations (2) and (3) exclude only the UK t statistics based on heteroscedastic-consistent (White) standard errors in parentheses. Equation (3) uses rail miles as an instrument for national product. All variables in logarithms. $F_c^{.05}(4,10) = 5.96$.

average. The telegraph network in the United Kingdom can be excused on the grounds that the quality of service was generally superior in the UK, of the cheapness and speed of the competing postal service, that investment in the system had been virtually stopped after 1866 when the nationalisation debate began in earnest or by a possible overstatement of UK income relative to other countries.[40] The earlier comparison with Belgium shows that the quality of service may explain at least some of the underprediction. Perhaps what is of most interest is that the differences in performance between Victorian state and private enterprise were small enough to be statistically insignificant. Each had their distinctive inefficiencies but the net effects were not so dissimilar.

V

The private industry did not perform ideally because the industry technology required some form of cooperation. The clustering of offices and the small number of messages per office indicates adverse effects of competition. Compared with a merger or with working arrangements, the form of co-operation chosen, the price cartel, was inefficient. A better organised private industry could have been achieved by a regulatory body which insisted on working arrangements between companies for traffic management. These arrangements would have offered incentives to eliminate excess capacity in populous areas and spread service to outlying regions. If companies could have used other firms' trunk lines at little more than cost, they would have been more inclined to develop facilities in areas where there were no competitors. They would have linked such areas into the national network and charged the appropriate price (generally higher than for routes joining large population centres). That solution is more historically implausible than a merger, the barrier to which was initially agreeing a value for the shares or property to be acquired. The 1863 Telegraph Act, which required the consent of the Board of Trade to the sale of any telegraph company, might have proved a stumbling block in view of the presumption in favour of competition, but there is no sign that the EITC saw it as such.

Those with an interest in nationalisation could therefore present a case that seemed disinterested. There were economies of scope to be gained from linking the post offices with the telegraph.[41] There were economies of integration that could be achieved by unitary control. The tariff issue was in principle entirely separate. The uniform tariff and the favourable terms for press traffic were in retrospect major arguments against nationalisation as it was undertaken. They were redistributions of income in favour of particular groups by means of pricing, an archetypal case of regulatory capture. If these manipulations, and the upwards pressure on wage costs, could have been resisted, then the massive expansion of traffic in the first few years of the Post Office regime shows that the state organisation might have offered a service that was more efficient than that of the private industry in the form adopted until 1868.

In fact the cost function evidence suggests the dominant private firm was more efficient than the later Post Office telegraph department in the sense that costs were driven down further as output expanded. A private (integrated) monopoly, without statutory barriers to entry, therefore was likely to have been socially preferable, on conventional cost-benefit analysis criteria, to the actual Post Office regime. As it was, telegraph users were subsidised by postal users which almost certainly involved a transfer from the poorer to the better off. If income distribution effects are ignored, then a case on efficiency grounds for the cross-subsidy may exist, but there seems to be no good reason to make that leap.

International comparison of the 1868 industry shows that the hypothesis that the private British industry performed neither better nor worse than other, mainly state and often subsidised industries, cannot be rejected. To modify and make more plausible Hamlet's maxim: 'Nothing's good or bad but comparison makes it so'. Both the private British industry and the Post Office telegraph can be shown to have been inefficient in comparison with theoretical ideal types. When they are compared with each other, or with how they might have been on the basis of the experience of other countries, warts and all, the difficulties of picking the better are enormous. Much easier is to prescribe improvements in the historical regime, which are typically anachronistic, although they may bear morals for later periods.

University of Hull

NOTES

An earlier version of this article was read as a paper at a Paris CNRS conference in 1987 and at Warwick University. The present form has been improved by the comments of participants and by those of an anonymous referee. Bob Millward also offered perceptive criticisms and is absolved from responsibility for remaining inadequacies.

1. R. Millward, 'The Emergence of Gas and Water Monopolies in 19th Century Britain: Why Public Ownership?', *Salford Discussion Paper in Economics* (1986).
2. J. Foreman-Peck, 'Natural Monopoly and Nineteenth Century Railway Policy', *Oxford Economic Papers*, 39, (1987), pp.699–718.
3. W.S. Jevons, 'On the Analogy between the Post Office, Telegraphs and Other Means of Conveyance of the United Kingdom as Regards Government Control', *Transactions of the Manchester Statistical Society* (1867), pp.89–104.
4. J.C. Kieve, *The Electrical Telegraph: A Social and Economic History* (Newton Abbot, 1973); G.W. Brock, *The Telecommunications Industry: The Dynamics of Market Structure* (Cambridge, MA, 1982); British Parliamentary Papers (1868), XLI, *Report to the Postmaster General by Mr Scudamore Upon the Proposals for Transferring to the Post Office the Control and Management of Electric Telegraphs Throughout the United Kingdom.*
5. BPP (1875), XX, *Report of a Committee Appointed by the Treasury to Investigate the*

Causes of the Increased Costs of the Telegraph Since the Acquisition of the Telegraphs by the State; BPP (1876), XIII, *Report from the Select Committee on the Post Office (Telegraph Department) Together with Proceedings of the Committee.*

6. Calculated from BPP (1867–68), XLI, *Supplementary Report to the Postmaster General Upon Proposals for Transferring to the Post Office the Control and Management of the Electric Telegraph*. For the experience of the US industry, see R.L. Thompson, *Wiring a Continent* (Princeton, NJ, 1947), and Brock op. cit.

7. BPP (1867–68), XLI, *Supplementary Report*, loc. cit., Appendix on Allen's Report.

8. *Prospectus and Directors' Report of the United Kingdom Telegraph Company July 1861*, Post Office Archives, Post 81/7.

9. BPP (1868), loc. cit.

10. Weaver Letter Book, p.39. Post Office Archives, Post 81/27.

11. Ibid., p.35.

12. Ibid., p.163.

13. Ibid., p.5.

14. Submarine Telegraph Co., *Report of Committee of Consultation*, February 1861, Post Office Archives, Post 81/105.

15. Weaver Letter Book, p.94.

16. BPP (1875), *Report of a Committee*, loc. cit., p.8.

17. A. Clinton, *Post Office Workers: A Trade Union and Social History* (London, 1984), pp.119–21; Kieve, op. cit., pp.185–7.

18. BPP (1876), loc. cit., *Report*, paras. 7, 40, 43, Evidence, qs. 1596, 1602.

19. BPP, *Report of the Postmaster General 1880*, pp.16–17.

20. *The Post Office: An Historical Summary* (HMSO, 1911), p.77; Kieve, op. cit., pp.193–5; Clinton, op. cit., pp.129–30.

21. G. Routh, 'Civil Service Pay, 1875–1950', *Economica* (Aug. 1954), pp.216, 222.

22. *The Post Office*, op. cit., pp.69, 77; Kieve, op. cit., Ch.11.

23. See, for example, the calculation assuming costs do not increase proportionately with messages in Sir J. Anderson, 'On the Statistics of Telegraphy', *Journal of the Statistical Society of London* (Sept. 1872), p.284. Brock believes scale economies were quickly exhausted but his discussion does not include all the overheads or system effects. G.W. Brock, *The Telecommunications Industry: The Dynamics of Market Structure* (Cambridge, MA, 1982).

24. G.J. Stigler, *The Organization of Industry* (Homewood, IL, 1968), Ch.7.

25. W.J. Baumol, 'Contestable Markets: An Uprising in the Theory of Industrial Structure', *American Economic Review*, 72 (1982), pp.1–15.

26. Some of the cost conditions and pricing behaviour that give rise to an unsustainable equilibrium are explained by W. Sharkey, *The Theory of Natural Monopoly* (Cambridge, 1982). Telser discusses in greater detail markets where co-operation has to replace competition. L.G. Telser, *A Theory of Efficient Co-operation and Competition* (Cambridge, 1987).

27. This is the Bertrand conjecture; that firms chose their prices on the assumption that other firms will not change theirs in response.

28. This is the Cournot conjectural variation. For an analysis of how there will be excessive entry into an industry composed of output choosing firms, see N.G. Mankiw and M.D. Whinston, 'Free Entry and Social Inefficiency', *Rand Journal of Economics*, 17 (1986), pp.48–59.

29. H. Hotelling, 'Stability in Competition', *Economic Journal*, 39 (1929), pp.41–57.

30. J. Bulow, J. Geanakopolos and P. Klemperer, 'Holding Idle Capacity to Deter Entry', *Economic Journal*, 95 (1985), pp.178–82.

31. Memorandum by the Director-General of the Belgian Telegraphs, Appendix No.1 to *Report from the Select Committee on the Electric Telegraph Bill*, BPP (1868), XI.

32. BPP, XXXVII, *Report by Mr Scudamore on The Reorganisation of the Telegraph Service of the United Kingdom* (1871), c.304, pp.22–3.

33. Ibid., pp.45–6.

34. The more extensive French system is described in M.J. Brown, *Report on the*

Working of the French Telegraphic System (HMSO, 1870), Post Office Archives, Post 83/66.

35. Wholesale price index from B.R. Mitchell, *Abstract of European Historical Statistics* (2nd ed., 1980). Wage index from Routh loc. cit., 'Manipulative A' series, adjusted to financial years and for the 1872 pay increase.

36. R. Price Williams, 'The Question of the Reduction of the Postal Telegraph Tariff', *Journal of the Statistical Society of London* (March 1881), pp.14–15.

37. Weaver Letter Book op. cit., 6 (Nov. 1866), p.132.

38. J. Foreman-Peck, 'The State and the Development of the Early European Telecommunications Network', *Histoire, Economie, Sociétés*, 4 (1988).

39. Telegraph subsidies in continental Europe raise some complex issues. If telegraph administrations were type 7 organisations, social welfare maximising monopolists with statutory barriers to entry, then in the presence of common costs they would subsidise traffic with the more price elastic demand by charging higher prices for the traffic with the less elastic demand. Belgium and Switzerland attained their high telegram usage rates by subsidising their domestic traffic with revenue from international and transit telegrams. The proposition that international telegram demand price elasticities were greater than national demand can most easily be tested on the data of the unitary French system for this period. Table 7 presents two different estimates of relative elasticities for the years 1860–80. Equations 7.1 and 7.2 show price elasticities of −1.86 for internal traffic and −0.86 for international. The dynamic formulations are presented in equations 7.3 and 7.4. These estimates are obtained from a first order error correction form of an OLS regression equation. This form has the advantage of implying a long-run equilibrium relationship while allowing the data to indicate the speed of adjustment towards that relationship. It also has the advantage of being more general than other models, such as partial adjustment, which have the same property. 7.3 and 7.4 give qualitatively similar results for the short run (year to year) relative elasticities; the international elasticity at −0.40 is one-half of the internal elasticity of −0.81. The long run elasticities are much closer. It is possible then that the cross subsidy between international and national traffic was socially efficient. In a potentially competitive industry, such as Britain's before the transfer, that policy cannot be pursued because it will be liable to encourage entry into the subsidising service. The social value of the widespread subsidy from the postal service is almost equally opaque. Here again there were common costs and different elasticities of demand. Hill's 'inverse square law', on which he based his unsuccessful projection of revenues from the 1840 price cut, was an assumption that the price elasticity of demand was −2. The persistence of reduced revenue for 13 years suggests the price elasticity for postal services was, instead, well below one, and the short run (year to year elasticity) was nearer one half. This figure is less than the price elasticity of demand for internal telegrams in either equation of Table 7. The theoretical argument for the cross subsidy requires either that compensation be paid to the losers from the arrangement or that consumers typically used both services. Since users of the postal service were not generally also prone to send telegrams and had lower incomes than those who seemed to benefit most from the telegraph industry, the theoretical argument is probably not applicable here.

40. The Crafts measure of British income per head (N.F.R. Crafts, 'Gross National Product in Europe 1870–1910: Some New Estimates', *Explorations in Economic History*, 20 (1983), pp.387–401) appears to be higher than Maddison's Table A2, A. Maddison, *Phases of Capitalist Development* (Oxford, 1982).

41. J. Foreman-Peck (1988), loc. cit.

Table 7

Demand for Internal and International Telegrams in France 1860-1880

Dep. Var.	Constant	Real Price	Real Income	War Dummy	Real Price	Real Income	Lagged Telegrams	$\bar{R}^2$	DW
1) Internal telegrams	-1.64 (-.43)	-1.86 (-8.02)	2.56 (2.67)	-.453 (-1.99)	-	-	-	.948	1.53
2) International telegrams	-15.93 (-4.29)	-.86 (-2.10)	5.97 (7.16)	.338 (1.45)	-	-	-	.809	1.88
3) Yearly change in internal telegrams	-1.37 (-.84)	-.14* (-1.17)	.67* (1.25)	-.23 (3.33)	-.81 (-8.36)	.26 (.65)	-.14 (1.71)	SSR .097	2.06
4) Yearly change in international telegrams	-2.22 (-1.25)	.21 (2.20)	.99 (1.73)	-.15 (2.28)	-.40 (3.69)	.50 (1.208)	.20 (2.52)	.107	1.78

Note: 1 and 2 estimated by OLS. 3 and 4 are estimated jointly by multivariate regression. t statistics in parentheses. * indicates variable lagged one period.

Sources: Telegrams and telegraph average revenue: *UK Statistical Abstract for Foreign Countries* (1881); real income, Maddison (1982) p.170, 172; general price index, Mitchell (1985).

THE BIRTH AND DEATH OF FIRMS IN ENGLAND AND WALES DURING THE INTER-WAR YEARS

By JOHN HUDSON

Business and economic historians are in considerable disagreement about the performance of British industry in the inter-war years. On the one hand there are those who see the high levels of unemployment and the decline of the staple industries as evidence of a declining economy. On the other hand there are those who see these old industries being replaced by new and more dynamic ones, in an example of what Schumpeter[1] has called creative destruction. This paper attempts to enter this debate from a relatively new perspective, with a data set which has been under-exploited by business historians. This is perhaps somewhat surprising as one of the principal problems confronting the quantitative business historian is poor quality data, particularly at the macro level. The data used here relate to company incorporations and liquidations and in fact stretch back to the middle of the nineteenth century, when the concept of the limited liability company was first introduced. In this article we shall be concerned solely with the inter-war years. Most limited liability companies were small private firms, in many cases partnerships or even one man businesses. Thus we shall be looking at this period not from the perspective of large or medium sized firms or industries which have tended to dominate previous analyses, but from that of the small entrepreneurial figure.

This lack of concern is reflected in economic theory. The firm plays a large and important part in economic theory, both micro and macro. It is, together with the consumer and the government, one of the three pillars on which modern analysis can be seen to rest. Because of this considerable effort has been directed at analysing corporate behaviour under a variety of market forms ranging from perfect competition to monopoly. Yet there has been relatively little work done on why firms come into and cease existence. Marshall[2] argued that in the absence of barriers to entry firms would be attracted into an industry if profits in that industry were above some 'normal' level. Similarly firms would eventually leave the industry if they were below this level. This work has subsequently been expanded upon by, for example, Bain.[3] However, this analysis is only superficially about the firm, as its main concern is with the efficiency of the market. Thus questions such as where do these firms come from and where they go to are largely ignored, and have only recently been examined.[4]

Figure 1 shows the number of companies registered during the period 1922–39, as well as the number liquidated during this period. The data relate to England and Wales only, as data for Scotland were not available until 1927. In the immediate post-war years both the number of newly registered companies and the number of liquidated companies were running at very high levels. To a certain extent this was still due to the influence of the war, and by 1921–22 the number of births had settled down to a more sustainable level. There was then only a small increase in this level until 1932 when the number of births began to increase quite sharply. This increase was sustained until a peak was reached in 1936. We have data on two kinds of liquidation, voluntary and compulsory, and the trends in these are rather different to that for births. From 1921 onwards there was a gradual decline in the number of companies going into voluntary liquidation until a sharp rise in 1928. Following this there is a gradual, although uneven, decline of which the trough in 1933–34 is the most notable feature. The data on compulsory liquidation follows a similar trend. But, there appears to be a two to three year lag between the two series. The sharp increase comes not in 1928 but two years later in 1930, whereas the trough previously noted for 1933–34 comes three years later in 1936–37.

However, the numbers of liquidations and births *per se* are slightly misleading as they give little idea of the incidence of company failures or the likely impact of new firms. For this liquidation and birth rates give a better guide. Figure 2 accordingly shows these rates, where both liquidations and births are measured as proportions of the number of companies on the register at the beginning of the year. Expressed in rates, the data for birth suggests the continuing strength of post-war incorporations and also the strength of the surge in births in the early to mid-1930s compared with the end of the decade. The compulsory liquidation rate was also very high in the early years of the 1920s and again during the early 1930s, especially 1930–32. Finally, the incidence of voluntary liquidation declines almost continously throughout the entire period. In evaluating these figures several points need to be borne in mind. First, not all firms which close down go through formal liquidation procedures. Many simply cease trading and are subsequently struck off the Register of Companies. Similarly not all new firms seek to become incorporated, many will set up as partnerships or sole traders. In addition, some firms which do register will simply be changing status from an unincorporated to a corporate form. Despite these qualifications, analysis of similar, but more recent, data has provided valuable insights and it is hoped that the same will be true here.

It is the task of this article to attempt to explain and reconcile these somewhat conflicting trends. In particular we shall seek to show why voluntary liquidations were declining and births increasing in the early 1930s, but compulsory liquidations were relatively high. The latter would seem to indicate a hostile economic environment for small firms, whilst the former would suggest otherwise. We shall begin the analysis

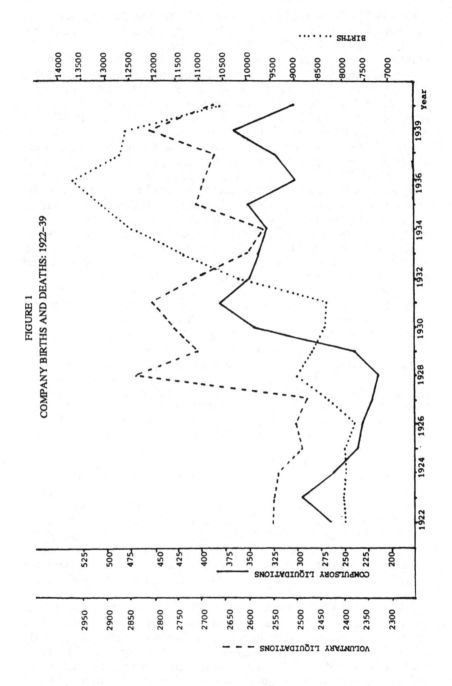

FIGURE 1
COMPANY BIRTHS AND DEATHS: 1922–39

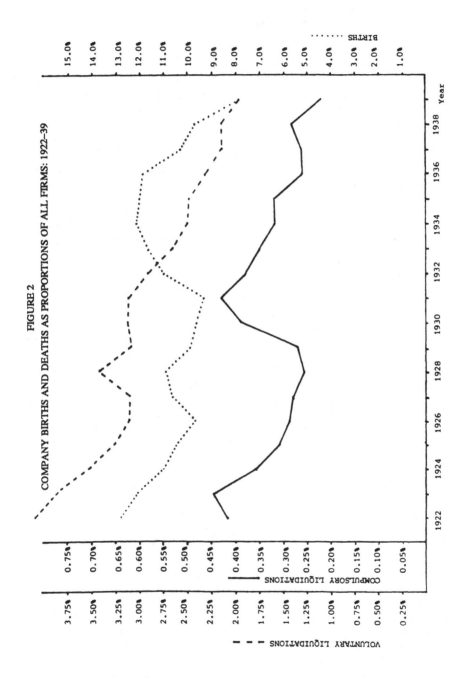

FIGURE 2
COMPANY BIRTHS AND DEATHS AS PROPORTIONS OF ALL FIRMS: 1922–39

with a theoretical section. Following this the results will be presented, and finally there will be a short conclusion.

I

Foreman-Peck[5] has recently published a detailed study of company births during the inter-war period. Much of the emphasis is on presenting a detailed analysis of trends at regional and industry levels. However, there is a multiple regression analysis based on a data-base derived from the Registry of Business Names. He includes amongst his independent variables profits, GDP, unemployment and a dummy variable related to the introduction of tariffs in 1932. Of these only unemployment is correctly signed and consistently significant across a range of regressions.

In a study of company births in the post-war period Hudson[6] has argued that an individual will set up in business if he expects to be better off than if he does not. An important factor in this is the comparison between the expected income gained from setting up in business compared with that from not setting up coupled with the degree of risk aversion. Most individuals will prefer a more certain income stream than one with greater possible variation. However, the degree of risk aversion can be expected to vary from individual to individual, and it may even be the case that some people have a preference for risk. The expected income gained from remaining as a paid employee is likely to be much more certain than the alternative and risk averse individuals will tend to prefer this option. The rate of time preference is also an important factor, it generally being assumed that people will prefer income now to income in the future. Because there will be an initial 'take-off' period when new entrepreneurs can expect their income to be below its long-run level, this would have been a further factor militating against the formation of new businesses. However, it may be that the individual can go on working longer as an entrepreneur than as an employee. This then is one factor which might lead to individuals, especially those approaching retiring age, setting up their own business.

There is one case where the expected non-entrepreneurial income stream can be as uncertain as that from setting up in business. This is when the individual is unemployed. In this case current income will equal any benefits received whilst unemployed. Future income will depend upon how soon he can expect to get a job and at what wage. Search theory would suggest that both of these factors will depend upon the number of relevant vacancies and the number of job searchers competing with him for those vacancies.[7] If we ignore on the job search, the latter can be proxied by the number of unemployed. The more vacancies and the fewer unemployed, the quicker he can expect to find a job and the higher also will be the expected wage at which it will be offered. Thus, both because of the greater uncertainty, the lower expected income stream and the fact that the bulk of this income stream is in the future, we would expect the probability of an individual setting up in business to increase if he becomes unemployed, and the more slack in the labour market the greater will be this increase. The possible role of unemployment in stimulating movement into business has long been realised by, for example, Schumpeter,[8] Oxenfeldt[9] and Steindl.[10] Whilst more recently Storey[11] and Johnson,[12] as well as Foreman-Peck,[13] have made similar arguments.

In many cases, whether the individual sets up in business or not may depend upon whether he can get the appropriate credit from the bank or some other agency. The bank's decision is likely to depend upon the rate of interest. Provided credit markets clear, then a rise in the general level of interest rates will reduce the net present value of the new firm's potential profits and make it less likely that new entrepreneurs will be able to get a loan from the bank. However, we shall be arguing later that there is some reason for believing that the market for credit does not clear, and in this case a rise in interest rates will coincide with riskier ventures being financed. New firms without any track record of success, possibly with unproven management in an unproven area, clearly fall into this category and in this case we might well see more of them being given credit following a rise in interest rates.

Hence, the probability that an individual will start a firm will be determined by the ratio of expected profits to current income, labour market conditions and the rate of interest. The profits expected from setting up a new firm may be linked to the average profitability of existing firms together with some variable proxying the number of potential opportunities for new businesses. In the empirical work which follows, real gross domestic product will be used for this. Data on vacancies is not available for much of the sample period, hence labour market conditions will be proxied by unemployment alone.

Finally, following Foreman-Peck, there is one further factor we should include in the analysis which stems from the particular circumstances of the 1930s. This is the introduction of tariff protection in 1931–32. By restricting foreign supplies this may well have left a gap in the market which might have encouraged the setting up of new firms, particularly in manufacturing. Foreman-Peck proxied this by constructing a dummy variable taking a value of unity from 1932 onwards and zero prior to that. This implies that the introduction of tariffs had a lasting impact upon the number of new firms being started every year. However, it is equally possible that its impact was more concentrated, and that once the gap in the supply side of the market had been filled by the inflow of new firms, the continuing impact of tariff restrictions upon the number of new firms coming into the market would be minimal. To model this possibility we shall construct a second dummy variable taking a value of unity in 1932 only and zeros everywhere else. We shall test for both of these variables in the empirical work.

Thus the equation we shall be estimating is

$$BIRNt = \alpha_0 + \alpha_1 U_t + \alpha_1 \pi_t + \alpha_3 Y_t + \alpha_4 r_t + \alpha_5 TD_t \qquad (1)$$

where $BIRN_t$ is the number of births in period t, U_t the level of unemployment, π_t a measure of profits, r_t the rate of interest, Y_t GDP and TD_t a tariff based dummy variable. It should be noted that unlike the other two equations we shall be estimating the dependent variable is not defined as a proportion of existing companies. It is valid to think of closure rates, but not of the birth rate. Closures obviously come from a subset of existing firms, new incorporations do not. It should also be noted that although we have specified all the above variables as being defined in period t, we shall also experiment with the inclusion of lagged values. One possible potential justification for the inclusion of lagged values is that it allows for inertia in the response of potential entrepreneurs to a changing state of the world, another is that it allows us to proxy expectations of the future. For example, expectations of the future GDP may be proxied by a weighed average of past values.

II

Compulsory Liquidations

Compulsory liquidations relate to companies which are forced into insolvency by the Court following a successful petition generally from one of the firm's creditors. It has been previously argued[14] that for creditors to press for closure, discounted profits must be less than the interest payments on the amount they would receive now if the firm were liquidated. Therefore the probability of a firm being pushed into bankruptcy by its creditors is a function of its cash position, its current indebtedness to the bank and its liquidation value. These are the factors which determine both whether the firm is likely to be in a situation of financial crisis and whether it is in the interests of creditors to press for immediate closure. The first two of these will depend upon recent profits. A situation of immediate financial crisis is likely to be preceded by negative trading profits. For simplicity we might also wish to make expected profits a function of current and past profits.

Faced with this situation the firm is likely to try and secure further credit from the bank. The bank may give this because the optimal decision for it differs to that for normal trade creditors. The firm can issue a debenture which gives the bank security in the form of a charge on its assets. This frequently takes the form of a charge, not on a fixed set of assets, but a floating charge. This device, virtually unique to English law, was devised by the Court of Chancery in the 1860s and its validity was first recognised by the Court of Appeals in Chancery in a case in 1870. It does not attach to any specific property but constitutes a charge upon assets which are constantly varying. The existence of such a security will ensure that in any liquidation the bank is ahead of other, unsecured, assets in the distribution of assets. Thus, the bank will extend a loan to the firm if it expects there to be some time in the future when, in discounted terms, the liquidation value of the firm is expected to exceed the total debt owed to the bank at that time plus any debt to preferential creditors. This decision will then be reviewed at the end of every time period.

An increase in general interest rate levels can be regarded as either increasing the payments due to the bank in future periods or further reducing the discounted future liquidation value of the firm. In any case it will reduce the likelihood that the bank will give credit to the firm. However, the analysis has been based on the assumption that the market for credit clears, and that interest rates are freely adjustable to cover all degrees of risk. Whereas, Jaffee and Modigliani,[15] Jaffee and Russell[16] and Keeton,[17] amongst others, argue that interest rates are not used to clear the market for credit. Some explain this by 'social conventions' forcing banks to charge a uniform rate to non-identical borrowers. Stiglitz and Weiss,[18] however, argue that the market clearing role of interest rates is diluted by its effect on the risk distribution of borrowers and upon existing borrowers' attitudes to risk. The interest rate a bank charges may itself affect the structure of the bank's loans by either discouraging low risk borrowers (the adverse selection effect) or affecting the actions of borrowers (the incentive effect). The adverse selection effect occurs because those who are most willing to pay high interest rates may, on average, be worse risks with a higher probability of default. The incentive effect arises because an increase in interest rates will decrease the return, in net present value terms, on projects which succeed, thus inducing firms to undertake projects with lower profitability of success but higher profits when successful. On both counts an increase in the rate of interest can be expected to increase the risk content of the bank's lending, and this will prevent it from fully using interest rates to equate demand and supply. They also argue that an increase in interest rates may result in only risky projects being financed. Thus in a situation where the bank rations credit between a number of would-be borrowers, a rise in interest rates will lead to a switch in credit towards borrowers with a low interest elasticity of demand. Firms facing insolvency fall into this category. Therefore, with rationing a rise in interest rates is likely, other things being equal, to lead to an increase in the number of distressed firms receiving credit facilities.

Thus the probability of a firm going into bankruptcy is determined primarily by past and current profits, together with the rate of interest. I shall assume that the former will be a function of aggregate profitability, its age and a vector of firm specific factors such as innate entrepreneurial ability and location. Age is likely to be important as a new firm is unlikely to reach an equilibrium level of profits immediately. The owners will be on a learning curve, where they find not only potential customers, but gain the knowledge necessary to run the business. Second, the fact that a company has been in existence a number of years is an indication that the owners are capable entrepreneurs and the industry is a viable one. Thus, age also acts a proxy for other firm specific factors. However, it takes time for a firm to build up debts, for creditors to perceive that the company cannot pay and for bankruptcy proceedings to begin. We might therefore also expect to see an initial 'honeymoon period' between a company being established and it getting into difficulties. Support for these hypotheses can be found in a study of the nineteenth century Lancashire cotton industry by Lloyd-Jones and Le Roux[19] who found that of the 57 firms under six years old in the 1815 population structure, 86 per cent were destined quickly to become exit firms. Similarly, Lomax[20] in a study of failures in New York between 1844 and 1926 showed that mortality was highest amongst new firms. Finally, Shannon[21] in a study of limited liability companies between 1866 and 1883, noted that for the formations of 1875–83 a tenth had become insolvent within three years of registration and one-seventh within five years. A further tenth wound up voluntarily within three years and something under a sixth within five years, and one in 12 were informally dissolved within three years and one in ten within five years. In all 29.7 per cent dissolved within three years and 40.1 per cent within five years.

In analysing company births it was argued that an unemployed worker would have been more likely to start a new firm than an employed worker. However, its prospects for success may be less than for other new firms. He may have set up in an industry or area which made it difficult for the firm to grow and survive. In many cases the expected profits would have been such that had the owner been in employment he would have not considered setting the firm up. In addition, such people were being forced into entrepreneurship, a role for which they may have been ill-suited. They may well, for example, have been more risk averse than entrepreneurs who give up paid employment to start a new firm. They may also have had less relevant experience. For all these reasons we might expect a particularly high failure rate amongst such firms. To allow for this we shall be including the average of unemployment (AU_t) in years t-1 to t-2 when analysing company failures in period t. Finally, again as with company births, the introduction of tariffs in 1932 may have had an impact upon the number of firms going into liquidation. In reducing competition, it should have made some firms which were previously at risk, less so. Indeed, initially the legislation was introduced more to protect existing firms, than to encourage the growth of new ones. Hence the equation we shall be estimating is:

$$LIQ_t = \beta_0 + \beta_1 AU_t + \beta_2 \pi_t + \beta_3 r_t + \delta_1(L)BIR_t + \beta_4 TD_t \qquad (2)$$

where $\delta_1(L)$ denotes a lagged operator.

Voluntary Liquidations

The term 'voluntary' is in fact something of a misnomer as the term simply refers to a firm which is being liquidated without recourse to the Court. It covers what was in the 1929 Companies Act to become two different classes of liquidation; creditors' voluntary liquidation and members' voluntary liquidation. The former relates to insolvent firms who choose to close down. There are several reasons why they should do so. First, the owners may anticipate that if they carry on trading they will be forced into liquidation by their creditors. Many of the factors which affect insolvencies will therefore also affect this category of liquidation. Second, they may be restricted by, for example, lack of finance or management skills in key areas, and accordingly seek to link themselves with a larger concern which can fill these gaps. Their decision will be determined by the total value of the package they can negotiate with a buyer. This may exceed the liquidation value of even a solvent firm, as included in the deal may be the entrepreneurial skills of the existing owners. None the less it is also likely to be linked to aggregate profitability. Such firms are unlikely to be very young firms, as it will take time for the business to be built up and its limitations to be perceived. On the other hand they are also unlikely to be old, established firms.

Third, there is the possibility that the owners may wish to retire, and if no suitable successor exists the firm will have to be liquidated. The timing of such liquidations may be related to profits in at least two different ways. First, the owners' willingness to continue may be greater during successful periods than unsuccessful ones. On the other hand, the liquidation value of the company is likely to be greater in the upswing than the downswing. Thus the exact nature of the short-run relationship with profits is not clear. Although in the long run this type of closure should be unrelated to profits. Finally, there is the possibility that the owners may choose to go into liquidation in the absence of insolvency or other problems, and with no intention of retiring or remaining with the firm if taken over. In this case they will need to seek alternative employment. There are two possibilities. They may attempt to set up another firm in a more profitable sector of the economy, or they may attempt to find paid employment as someone's elses employee.

In order for owners to go into liquidation and seek paid employment two conditions need to be satisfied. First, the net discounted earnings of doing so must exceed the net discounted earnings of not going into liquidation. Labour market conditions, in determining likely earnings in paid employment, are once more an important factor in this decision. Second, they must also exceed the net discounted earnings of going into liquidation and transferring to the most profitable alternative industry. If the first of these conditions holds, but not the second, then the owners will transfer to this industry instead. In this case a liquidation may not result as the shift can take place within the existing corporate structure. Indeed the objects clause of the articles of association are frequently drawn so wide that not even this may need to be changed.

It will take some years for the owners of an unsuccessful firm to realise that their income is not going to reach an acceptable level, and to consider voluntary liquidation. This lag is a further example of a honeymoon period. Its length will be determined by the amount of time it takes expectations to adapt to reality. After this we would expect to see a relatively high proportion of firms being voluntarily liquidated. This period of high liquidation risk will last for several years as some owners may be slow to adapt their expectations and some firms will be only marginally unprofitable. Thus the equation for voluntary liquidations is

$$\text{VOL}_t = \Gamma_0 + \Gamma_1 \text{AU}_t + \Gamma_2 \text{U}_t + \Gamma_3 \pi_t + \Gamma_4 r_t + \delta_2(\text{L})\text{BIR}_t + \Gamma_5 \text{TD}_t \qquad (3)$$

The inclusion of the two unemployment variables reflects the dual nature of the dependent variable. AU_t, as in equation (2), is included to reflect the possibility that firms started by unemployed workers are more likely subsequently to become insolvent. U_t is included to reflect the influence of the state of the labour market on the decisions to close down and seek paid employment.

III

Equations (1)–(3) were estimated by both ordinary least squares and seemingly unrelated regressions (SURE). The results are shown in Table 1. Turning first to equation (1a) which relates to company births, all the variables, apart from the constant term, are significant at the five per cent level and both profits, and the rate of interest and unemployment are significant at the one per cent level. In addition the explanatory power of the equation is quite high. The coefficients of GDP and GDP lagged one year were nearly equal in absolute terms, but oppositely signed. This suggests that it is not the level of GDP which is important for company births, but the change in GDP (CGDP), and it is this single variable which is used in all the relevant questions in Table 1. This is also the only major difference between these results and those for the post-Second World War period.[22] It also gives a new perspective on the accelerator theory whereby an increase in output requires increased productive capacity and therefore results in increased investment. In this case the increased capacity is provided by the growth of new firms.

The effect of adding the tariff dummy variable to this equation is shown in equation (1b). This is significant at the five per cent level, and suggests that the introduction of tariffs increased the number of new firms by 1664 per annum throughout the rest of the 1930s. The significance of the other variables declines, which may well be the result of multicollinearity, although the only variable which is insignificant at

TABLE 1

REGRESSION RESULTS: 1922–39

	Eqn. 1a	Eqn. 1b	Eqn. 1c	Eqn. 2a	Eqn. 2b	Eqn. 2c	Eqn. 3a	Eqn. 3b	Eqn. 3c
Dependent Variable	Births	Births	Births	Com Liq	Com Liq	Com Liq	Vol Liq	Vol Liq	Vol Liq
Constant	-6047	-1158	-3947	0.240	0.178	0.228	3.536	2.580	2.583
	(2.73)	(0.41)	(1.88)	(1.62)	(1.08)	(2.30)	(5.66)	(5.01)	(6.41)
Profits	1015	696	879	-0.0117	-0.0097	-0.0125	-0.259	-0.162	-0.164
	(6.38)	(3.62)	(6.06)	(1.13)	(0.99)	(1.88)	(6.67)	(4.21)	(5.46)
interest rate	-116	-69.0	-86.8	0.00701	0.00609	0.00696	0.0504	0.0413	0.0413
	(3.29)	(1.90)	(3.02)	(2.88)	(2.30)	(4.06)	(5.81)	(6.23)	(7.96)
unemployment	464	258	366	0.00801	0.01097	0.00883	-0.0553	-0.0158	-0.0164
	(6.22)	(2.37)	(4.65)	(1.70)	(1.43)	(2.56)	(3.75)	(1.04)	(1.39)
CGDP	256	127	128						
	(2.38)	(1.18)	(1.63)						
Trade dummy		1664	1019		-0.0249			-0.383	-0.379
		(2.36)	(1.99)		(0.49)			(3.60)	(4.56)
Births 1 period ago				-0.00185			0.155	0.137	0.140
				(0.10)			(2.54)	(3.15)	(4.11)
Births 2 periods ago				0.0116	0.0123	0.0111	0.101	0.087	0.087
				(1.51)	(1.58)	(1.99)	(3.95)	(4.72)	(6.03)
R²	0.902	0.933	0.924	0.688	0.694	0.686	0.950	0.977	0.977
DW	1.87	1.43	1.40	1.29	1.17	1.29	1.65	2.43	2.43
Critical t value at 5% significance	2.145	2.160	2.160	2.160	2.160	2.145	2.160	2.179	2.179
Critical t value at 10% significance	1.761	1.771	1.771	1.771	1.771	1.761	1.771	1.782	1.782
F statistic		4.37	3.55	8.45	7.49	10.16	67.32	27.04	38.43
Critical F		(3.18)	(3.18)	(3.41)	(3.41)	(3.34)	(3.41)	(3.49)	(3.49)
Technique	OLS	OLS	SUR	OLS	OLS	SUR	OLS	OLS	SUR

Notes: 1. For compulsory liquidations the unemployment variable is the average level of unemployment in the two previous periods. For voluntary liquidations and births it is the level of unemployment in the current period. 2. Figures in parentheses are t statistics, R^2 are unadjusted for degrees of freedom. 3. All regressions are based on 19 observations.

the ten per cent level is the change in GDP. This potential problem of multicollinearity is reflected in the relatively high correlations between the tariff dummy and the other variables shown in Table 2. The tariff dummy reported in the equations is operative from 1932 onwards. The second tariff dummy operative for 1932 only did not improve the regressions in any of the three cases. Thus it must be concluded that at the very least the supply side gap opened up by tariffs took some years to fill.

TABLE 2

CORRELATION MATRIX BETWEEN DEPENDENT
AND INDEPENDENT VARIABLES

Variable	V.L	C.L.	Births	Gdp	Cgdp	Profits	Unemp	interest rate	Birl1	Birl2	Tariff dummy	Av unemp
Vol Liq	1.000	0.647	-0.825	-0.912	-0.256	-0.615	-0.047	0.832	0.094	0.411	-0.839	-0.411
Com Liq	0.647	1.000	-0.424	-0.686	-0.380	-0.465	0.549	0.745	0.100	0.276	-0.354	0.106
Births	-0.825	-0.424	1.000	0.737	0.386	0.704	0.187	-0.597	0.272	-0.149	0.918	0.638
Gdp	-0.912	-0.686	0.737	1.000	0.376	0.745	-0.201	-0.754	-0.100	-0.262	0.711	0.134
Cgdp	-0.256	-0.380	0.386	0.376	1.000	0.501	-0.468	-0.232	0.357	0.186	0.346	0.161
Profits	-0.615	-0.465	0.705	0.745	0.501	1.000	-0.411	-0.418	0.488	0.067	0.561	0.134
Unemp	-0.047	0.549	0.187	-0.201	-0.468	-0.411	1.000	0.109	-0.250	-0.160	0.290	0.590
interest rate	0.832	0.745	-0.597	-0.754	-0.232	-0.413	0.109	1.000	0.187	0.233	-0.549	-0.113
Birl1	0.094	0.100	0.272	-0.100	0.357	0.488	-0.250	0.187	1.000	0.125	0.071	0.313
Birl2	0.411	0.276	-0.149	-0.262	0.186	0.067	-0.160	0.233	0.125	1.000	-0.227	-0.385
Trade dummy	-0.839	-0.355	0.918	0.711	0.346	0.561	0.290	-0.549	0.071	-0.227	1.000	0.713
Av unemp	-0.411	0.107	0.638	0.135	0.161	0.134	0.590	-0.113	0.313	-0.385	0.713	1.000

Notes: The abbreviated variable names are (i) Vol Liq, voluntary liquidations, (ii) Com Liq, compulsory liquidations, (iii) Cgdp, the change in GDP, (iv) unemp. unemployment, (v) Birl1, the birth rate 1 year previously, (vi) Birl2, the birth rate two years previously.

Turning to compulsory liquidations, as shown in equation (2a), the results are less satisfactory, only the rate of interest is signficant at the ten per cent level. In addition, the overall explanatory power of the regression is not as good as in the other equations. These less than satisfactory results may be due to the lengthy lags involved with this class of liquidation. Not only are there the problems of instigating legal proceedings, but previous research[23] on companies liquidated over the period 1978–81 has shown that many of the companies involved in a compulsory liquidation had first to be restored to the Register of Companies before legal proceedings could begin. In many cases the petitioner was a government body, such as Customs and Excise, who take a long time to respond to bad debts. Thus a company being compulsorily liquidated may in fact have ceased trading one or two years previously. The introduction of the tariff dummy variable does not significantly alter matters, with it also being insignficant at the ten per cent level.

Equation (3a) in Table 1 shows the result of estimating the voluntary liquidations equation by OLS. Here all the variables are significant at the one per cent level, except births lagged one period which is significant at the five per cent level, and again the explanatory power of the equation is reasonably high. In this case we find the trends of unemployment, the real rate of interest and profits tend to favour fewer liquidations. The unemployment variable is the current level rather than a moving average of past levels, the latter proving insignificant. This suggests that worsening job search conditions were a more important factor in reducing voluntary exits, than declining entre-preneurial ability was in increasing insolvencies. The result of adding the tariff dummy variable to this equation is shown in equation (3b). Again it is significant, this time at the one per cent level. However, unemployment is now insignificant at the ten per cent level, although once more this may be due to the existencee of multicollinearity.

However, it is probable that OLS is not the most efficient technique to analyse these equations as it is likely that the error terms in the three equations are correlated over time. Random shocks can be expected to affect both categories of liquidation in a similar manner, and possibly also affect new registrations. An event which increases the number of insolvencies might also be expected to reduce the number of new registrations. Thus we would expect the error terms between the compulsory liquidations' and births' equations to be negatively correlated. The relationship between these two error terms and that from the voluntary liquidations equation is not so clear. We would expect that part of this error term which is related to insolvencies to be positively correlated to compulsory liquidations and negatively to births. However, the reverse may be the case for that part stemming from solvent liquidations. Seemingly unrelated regressions (SURE) take account of any such correlations, therefore yielding more efficient estimates than OLS. However, we shall not be presenting the results derived from using Zellner's[24] original method, but from a more efficient maximum likelihood procedure found in both RATS and TSP.[25] Use of Zellner's original technique did not significantly alter the results. Equations (1c), (2c) and (3c) in Table 1 illustrate the improve-ment in efficiency. The voluntary liquidations equation in particular has improved substantially and all the coefficients are now correctly signed and significant at the one per cent level, apart from unemploy-ment which is now only marginally below the ten per cent level of significance and the tariff dummy which is significant at that level. But it is equation (2c) relating to compulsory liquidations which has seen the most substantial improvement, unemployment, and the rate of interest are now both significant at the five per cent level of significance and protifs and births lagged two years only just fail to be so, although both are signficant at the 10 per cent level.

It is possible that liquidations, particularly voluntary liquidations, were affected by legislative changes. The principal such change was, of course, the Companies Act in 1929, which distinguished between solvent and insolvent firms going into voluntary liquidation. This legislation may, for example, have led to a change in the balance between the number of firms going into voluntary liquidation and compulsory liquidation. It might also have had a short term anticipatory effect by which ailing firms choose to go into voluntary liquidation before the act came into effect. In this case we would not only expect an increase in voluntary liquidations in 1928 which Figures 1 and 2 indicate as a clear possibility, but also a decline in the following year. We constructed several dummy variables to test for these possibilities. There was no indication of any long-term change in the balance between compulsory and voluntary liquidations. A dummy variable operative for 1928 did prove very significant in the voluntary liquidations equation when estimated by seemingly unrelated regressions. However, there was no indication of a corresponding decline in 1929. Thus, whilst there is some evidence for an anticipatory effect, this is not conclusive. The effect of including this variable in the equation, the result of which is not shown in Table 1 due to lack of space, is to increase the significance of the other variables. In particular unemployment which was previously insignificant now becomes significant. Thus whilst there is some evidence for the anticipatory impact of legislative change on voluntary liquidations, this possibility does not dilute the significance of the other variables.

The F statistic at the end of each equation is derived from the test for the significance of additional explanatory variables. In this case we are testing the significance of the economic or cyclical variables as a whole. There is no such statistic for equation 1a because only economic variables appear in this equation. For equation 1b, however, the F statistic relating to the improvement of fit from including profits, the rate of interest, unemployment and the change in GDP in the regression is 4.37. The critical F statistic at the five per cent level is 3.18, as is shown immediately below the F statistic. Thus we can conclude that in addition to their individual significance, the cyclical variables as a whole are significant. This is also the case for all the remaining equations in Table 1.

Table 3 helps in the interpretation of the regressions by decomposing the changes in births and liquidations into the different causes as estimated by the seemingly unrelated set of regressions. Turning to births we can see that in 1928, for example, 1,213 more firms were incorporated than in 1926. This increase was due to two main factors: an improvement in profits and an increase in GDP, which led to about 959 and 541 more incorporations respectively. Countering this effect, however was a decline in unemployment and an increase in interest rates which respectively led to some 480 and 382 fewer firms being incorporated. The reason that the sum of the individual effects does not equal the total change in births is due to a random error term. As we progress through the 1930s we find the number of incorporations steadily increases beyond the 1926 figure. In general all the individual factors helped in this, but most important were the increase in profitability and, in the early part of the 1930s, the rise in unemployment. Also important was the introduction of tariffs which tended to result in slightly more than an extra 1,000 incorporations every year.

The second part of this table deals with compulsory liquidations. We can see that just 16 fewer firms went into liquidation in 1928 than 1926. This reduction was largely due to an improvement in profits which reduced liquidations by 11 and also a reduction in births lagged two periods which reduced liquidations by almost five. The reason the sum of the individual effects does not equal the total change in liquidations is again partly due to the effects of a random error term. However, more important is the fact that both types of liquidation are modelled as rates or proportions of the total number of companies. The number of companies going into liquidation may change even if the liquidation rate does not provided the total number of companies change. In this case the total number of companies was increasing throughout the period; hence in general the change in the number of liquidations will exceed that implied by the change in the liquidation rate. Finally, turning to voluntary liquidations we see that throughout the period as a whole profits, unemployment and interest rates all tended to reduce liquidations below their 1926 level, with increased profitability being particular important by 1936. The combination of these three factors is why voluntary liquidation rates declined steadily throughout this period. But again, the steady increase in the total number of companies negated this effect leading to the number of companies going into voluntary liquidation showing a slight increase over the 1926 level.

Thus it can be seen that this research has pointed to several factors which helped reduce the number of liquidations and increase the number of incorporations in the 1930s. Two of these were the direct consequence of government policy decisions. Low interest rates and the introduction of tariff barriers were active factors in both increasing the number of new incorporations and reducing the number of deaths. Moreover the significance of interest rates in this manner clearly suggests that credit markets did clear in the inter-war period, that is that interest rates were being used to equate the demand and supply for credit. This implies that there was no credit rationing in the sense of firms or other economic agents unable to obtain loans at the going rate of interest. It also implies that the cheap money policies of the 1930s were successful in generating the growth of new firms. Low real interest rates in this sense were an 'active' ingredient in economic recovery rather than the 'passive' one Alford[26] and others have suggested. The improvement in profitability and the increase in unemployment may be directly linked. Neither were a direct consequence of government policy, but their significance in promoting new firm growth does

TABLE 3

DECOMPOSITION OF CHANGES IN LIQUIDATIONS AND BIRTHS INTO
DIFFERENT CAUSES, WITH 1926 AS THE BASE YEAR

The determinants of changes in births from 1926

Year	Total	profits	unempl-oyment	interest rates	change in gdp	tariff dummy
1928	1213	958.52	-479.8	-381.64	541.09	0.0
1930	607	568.39	885.8	3.4800	382.72	0.0
1932	2403	-364.05	2509.7	-450.68	448.71	1004.3
1934	4672	1527.2	1144.1	223.93	976.60	1004.3
1936	5940	3567.3	221.4	165.55	673.06	1004.3

The determinants of changes in compulsory liquidations from 1926

Year	Total	profits	unempl-oyment	interest rates	births (t-2)
1928	-16.000	-11.239	1.8270	25.222	-4.735
1930	114.00	-7.0820	-1.1650	-0.2450	2.970
1932	118.00	4.7740	45.781	33.314	-8.807
1934	100.00	-22.238	66.260	-18.378	0.176
1936	70.000	-58.365	39.775	-15.267	10.94

The determinants of changes in voluntary liquidations from 1926

Year	Total	profits	unempl-oyment	interest rates	births (t-1)	births (t-2)	tariff dummy
1928	340.00	-165.82	19.432	142.88	17.6450	-41.585	0.0
1930	257.00	-104.50	-38.124	-1.3900	-23.9690	26.084	0.0
1932	209.00	70.440	-113.69	188.72	-149.770	-77.347	-292.87
1934	65.000	-328.11	-57.544	-104.11	184.110	-1.5470	-325.17
1936	190.00	-861.13	-12.514	-86.490	257.840	96.068	-365.37

Source: These figures were derived by multiplying the regression coefficients reported in Table 1 by the relevant changes in the variables.

suggest that this is one of the ways the macro-economy returns to full employment equilibrium following a large recession. This does not mean that Keynesian type policies are unnecessary, nor that governments need not interfere on the supply side to make it easier for small firms to survive and grow, as such policies may still speed up the return to equilibrium. These are points we will return to in the conclusion.

IV

The nature of the inter-war period has been the subject of debate between business and economic historians seeking to characterise it as a period of either dynamic growth or of waste and inefficiency. This research has concentrated on an aspect of this debate which, the article by Foreman-Peck apart, has previously been ignored; that is, the development of limited liability companies. These are generally small private companies, frequently partnerships or even one-man businesses. Foreman-Peck's article concentrated upon an analysis of company births at regional and industry levels. The present paper has differed from the work by Foreman-Peck in two respects. First, it has considered company deaths as well as births. Second, it has laid the emphasis on a time series analysis.

The results indicate that the rapid increase in new firm formations which took place from 1932 onwards was partially caused by an increase in profitability and by a decline in real interest rates. However, two further factors of major importance were the rise in the level of unemployment and the introduction of tariffs in 1932. The latter does seem to have both increased the number of new firms starting up as well as reducing the number going into liquidation. Although it should be borne in mind that it is possible that the international growth of trade restrictions had an impact upon GDP growth which was unfavourable to small companies. The unemployed can be seen to have been seeking their own solution to their problem. In this sense the depression carried the seeds of self correction, with a semi-automatic shift towards a more entrepreneurial, small firm, based economy. However, it would appear that many of the firms set up by the unemployed were subsequently to fail, either because the business was basically unsound, or alternatively because the unemployed 'forced' into entrepreneurship were unsuited to the task. Overall, however, this was a period which saw the number of limited liability firms grow at a much faster rate than in the past, as Table 4 shows. During the period 1922–30 the average annual rate of growth of such firms was 3.91 per cent. In the period 1930–38 this jumped to 5.26 per cent. Moreover, as the table also shows, this rate of increase is much faster than throughout the post-Second World War period. The combination of low interest rates and high profits coupled with tariff protection and high unemployment were sufficient to ensure that the 1930s were highly favourable for the growth and survival of small firms.

TABLE 4

THE GROWTH OF LIMITED LIABILITY COMPANIES

Period	Annual rate of increase in the number of limited liability companies
1922-30	3.91%
1930-38	5.26%
1950-60	4.46%
1960-70	3.29%
1970-80	4.56%
1980-84	4.30%

Source: Derived from various issues of the Board of Trade Companies General Annual Report.

The major difference between these econometric results compared with those of the post-Second World War period lies in the influence of interest rates. In the present study the hypothesis that credit markets do not clear has been rejected. An increase in real interest rates tended to reduce the number of new incorporations and increase the number of closures. Whereas in the more recent period some evidence did emerge to support the non-market clearing hypothesis. Apart from this, the main results are similar to those for this more recent period. The significance of profits, the existence of a honeymoon period followed by one of high risk, and the importance of unemployment are all consistent with this later period.

School of Social Sciences,
University of Bath

APPENDIX
Data Sources and Definitions

$BIRN_t$ The number of company registrations[a].

BIR_{t-i} The number of company registrations in period t-i as a proportion of the number of companies in existence at the beginning of year t[a].

LIQ The proportion of total companies on the Register at the beginning of the year going into compulsory liquidation[a].

VOL The proportion of total companies on the Register at the beginning of the year going into voluntary liquidation. It should be noted that this includes both solvent and insolvent firms[a].

$\pi = $(Net Profit/Net GNP)*100. Profits divided by GNP at factor cost[c].

r   The real rate of interest defined as the rate on short dated gilt edged yields less the rate of inflation in the previous year[b].

Y   Real GDP at factor cost, £bn, 1980 prices[b].

CGDP The annual change in real GDP.

U   The number of unemployed expressed as a percentage of the estimated total number of employees in employment plus the unemployed[b].

AU The average of unemployment, as defined above, in the previous two years[b].

TD A dummy variable, reflecting the introduction of tariffs. It takes a value of 1 from 1932 onwards and a zero otherwise.

Sources: a: Various issues of the Board of Trade Companies General Annual Report;
b: *Economic Statistics, 1900–1983* (London, *Economist*, 1985);
c: *The British Economy, Key Statistics 1900–1970* (London, London and Cambridge Economic Service, 1972).

NOTES

I would like to acknowledge the helpful comments of two anonymous referees.

1. J.A. Schumpeter, *Business Cycles, A Theoretical, Historical and Statistical Analysis of the Capitalist Process*, 2 vols. (New York, 1939).
2. A. Marshall, *Principles of Economics* 8th ed. (London, 1920).
3. J.S. Bain, *Barriers to New Competition* (Cambridge, 1956).
4. Principally by J.S. Foreman-Peck, 'Seedcorn or Chaff? New Firm Foundation and the Performance of the Interwar Economy', *Economic History Review*, Vol.XXXVIII, No.3 (1985), pp.402–22.
5. Foreman-Peck, ibid.
6. J. Hudson, 'Company Births in Great Britain', *International Small Business Journal*, Vol.VI, No.1 (1987), pp.58–9.
7. See J. Hudson, *Unemployment After Keynes: Towards a New General Theory* (Hemel Hempstead, 1988), pp.22–7.
8. Schumpeter, op. cit., p.94.
9. A.R. Oxenfeldt, *New Firms and Free Enterprise* (Washington, 1943), pp.120–23.
10. J. Steindl, *Small and Big Business* (Oxford, 1945), p.61.
11. D.J. Storey, *Entrepreneurship and the New Firm* (London, 1982), p.112.
12. P. Johnson, *New Firms: An Economic Perspective* (London, 1986), pp.75–6.
13. Foreman-Peck, op. cit., p.404.
14. See J. Hudson, 'An Analysis of Company Liquidations', *Applied Economics*, Vol.18, No.2 (1986), pp.221–2.
15. D. Jaffee and F. Modigliani, 'A Theory and Test of Credit Rationing', *American Economic Review*, Vol.LIX, No.4 (1969), pp.850–72.
16. D. Jaffee and F. Russell 'Imperfect Information and Credit Rationing', *Quarterly Journal of Economics*, Vol.XC, No.4 (1976), pp.651–66.
17. W. Keeton, *Equilibrium Credit Rationing* (New York, 1979).
18. J. Stiglitz and A. Weiss, 'Credit Rationing in Markets with Imperfect Information', *American Economic Review*, Vol.71, No.3 (1981), pp.393–410.
19. R. Lloyd-Jones and A.A. Le Roux, 'Marshall and the Birth and Death of Firms: the Growth and Size Distribution of Firms in the Early Nineteenth-Century Cotton Industry', *Business History*, Vol.XXIV, No.2 (1982), p.145.
20. K.S. Lomax, 'Business Failures. Another Example of the Analysis of Failure Data', *Journal of the American Statistical Association*, Vol.49, No.268 (1954), pp.847–52.
21. H.A. Shannon, 'Limited Companies of 1866–83' *Economic History Review*, Vol.4 (1933), reprinted in E.M. Carus-Wilson (ed.), *Essays in Economic History* (London, 1954), pp.380–405.
22. See Hudson, 'Company Births', op. cit.
23. See J. Hudson, 'Structure of Company Liquidations', *Journal of British Finance and Accounting*, Vol.14, No.2 (1987), p.211.
24. A. Zellner, 'An Efficient Method of Estimating Seemingly Unrelated Regressions and Tests for Aggregation Bias', *Journal of the American Statistical Association*, Vol.57, No.298 (1962), pp.348–68.
25. RATS and TSP are econometric package programmes. RATS stands for regression analysis of time series and TSP time series processor.
26. B.W.E. Alford, *Depression and Recovery? British Economic Growth 1918–1939* (London, 1975), p.38.

LOCATIONAL CHOICE, PERFORMANCE AND THE GROWTH OF BRITISH MULTINATIONAL FIRMS

By STEPHEN NICHOLAS

Introduction

Five years ago it was possible to write that British foreign direct investment (FDI) was a neglected area of business history research.[1] This is no longer true. The study of the multinational firm is one of the most dynamic fields of economic history and business historians have made remarkable progress in the study of the origins, growth and performance of Britain's largest multinational enterprises (MNEs).[2] Almost exclusively this new research has adopted the case study approach, the traditional business history methodology. The hallmark of the case study is the detailed archival research and firm-specific explanations of firm growth and performance. But, no matter how carefully researched and valuable in their own right, case studies rarely allow generalisations to be drawn for the growth and performance of all MNEs in the economy. However, by combining together a number of individual studies it might be possible to generalise about the growth process of the wider population of all British MNEs.

So far few attempts have been made to aggregate case studies, and such aggregate samples are not without problems.[3] For example, aggregate samples biased towards the large and successful firms would not be representative of the population of all pre-1939 British multi-nationals. Generalisations drawn from such non-random samples may be no more robust than those derived from the study of a single firm.[4] A further serious drawback is that samples derived from case studies do not allow quantitative analysis. The rigorous requirements of minimal sample sizes and random sampling for statistical estimation mean that samples of five, ten or even 15 firms are not amenable to econometric testing. As a result, the reliance on case studies or small samples of case studies means that such basic parameters as the geographic location, the timing and the form of British FDI are unknown.

In spite of such lacunae, a consensus view has developed about the location and performance of British FDI. Historians have adjudged the performance of Britain's pre-1939 multinationals as 'poor'. In a paper based on the experience of Dunlop, Courtaulds and Cadbury, Geoffrey Jones concluded that most MNEs were not successful in their overseas ventures.[5] Using an expanded sample of eight firms, a group of business historians at the LSE confirmed Jones' conclusion, presenting a virtual compendium of multinational failure.[6] The proponents of failure acknowledge that their case rests on select examples, without adequate confirming quantitative evidence. Complaints by directors of disappointing profit levels and poor performance skimmed from the board minutes forms a tenuous base upon which to erect a case of multinational failure. There has been no attempt to compare performance across firms in the same industry or to compare British multinationals with their American and European counterparts. Nor have absolute standards of performance been established with which the actual performance of British MNEs can be compared.

Nevertheless, the case of failure has been widely accepted, and much energy has been devoted to analysing the causes of the alleged poor performance of British MNEs. One explanation focuses on inadequate management. Following an hypothesis first propounded by Alfred Chandler, business historians claimed that the persistence of family control explained the slow development of modern management structures with deficient top management procedures and poorly trained managers and marketing specialists.[7] As a result, parent firms gave their overseas branches a loose and free rein, with periodic visits by a home-based family director the usual form of control. This lack of managerial control, Jones argued, lay at the root of the poor economic performance of the British multinational.[8] Whatever the plausibility of the argument, in the one test of the managerial failure thesis, Roy Church concluded that neither the strength or weakness in the performance of British international motor companies could be inferred from family control.[9]

Recently, Mira Wilkins suggested that the size of the home market explained much of the failure of British MNEs to develop appropriate management structures.[10] In the large American market, American managers of interregional companies learned how to manage multiregional operations by evolving managerial hierarchies to control production, marketing and distribution. Britain's small and homogeneous home market did not offer similar opportunities to British managers and, as Leslie Hannah has shown, British domestic firms only slowly adopted the new central functional departmental structure which allowed managers to control geographically dispersed operations.[11] Unfortunately, it was these new management structures, denied to British MNEs by the small domestic market, which served American multinationals so well in their overseas expansion.

Managerial failure was reflected most clearly in poor overseas marketing. According to Chandler the partial and hesitant vertical integration into marketing at home left British firms competitively weak internationally, a view endorsed by Jones who identified poor marketing and selling as a cause of the poor performance by British MNEs.[12] This emphasis on managerial failure merges with the old literature which identified entrepreneurial failure between 1870 and 1939 with inefficient marketing and selling abroad. The evidence on entrepreneurial failure rested largely on the 1899 consular-based

Report on Foreign Trade Competition, which provided a checklist of British selling failures, including the failure to study customers' wishes, to adopt the metric system, to grant credit facilities, to learn foreign languages and to send travellers abroad.

While rarely criticising and probing the accuracy of the consular reports themselves, the critics of British selling faithfully reported the alleged entrepreneurial failures. For example, Derek Aldcroft argued that 'if Britain was behind the times in techniques and methods of production, she was even further behind in her selling methods'.[13] David Landes complained that British industry abroad was complacent and amateurish, with firms taking export markets for granted, refusing to suit goods to clients, unwilling to try new products, and insistent that everyone should count in pounds, shilling and pence.[14] In an analysis of the decline of British economic power, Kirby and Lewis both criticised British firms for having few commercial travellers, crude and amateurish selling and poor credit facilities.[15] The case against the entrepreneur merged with the managerial failure explanations when Peter Payne, in his analysis of British entrepreneurship, identified the small size of the family firm as the reason that Britain could not afford vigorous selling and marketing forces abroad.[16]

Recently, Nicholas argued that there was little evidence that British overseas marketing performance was amateurish and inefficient before 1914.[17] In terms of product promotion, advertising, travelling, assembly, repair and after-sale service British firms competed on an equal footing with their German and American counterparts. The establishment of overseas selling branches heralded the triumph of marketing over production in British industry. With the founding of a sales branch, mercantile houses, agents and franchises were replaced by the firm's own salaried salesmen and managers resident in the host country. The sales branch allowed the more intensive use of marketing methods, including new product launches, trade and press advertising, souveniers, posters and catalogues, demonstrations, and brand name advertising. More importantly, the sales branch allowed an expanded after-sale service and credit financing facilities compared to the agency and mercantile systems. In addition, the sales branch was the first step in the FDI process; selling became the foundation upon which overseas production was built. With a fully integrated sales and production facility in a host country, the British MNE had a powerful institutional device for competing internationally.

Some evidence of how eagerly British firms utilised the MNE as a marketing device was the prolific establishment of overseas sales and production branches. In the period before 1939 there were over 400 British manufacturing multinationals, easily outnumbering the combined total of their American and European counterparts. British multinationals were widespread geographically and British FDI spanned the whole product range. Surprisingly, business historians have intepreted the establishment of overseas branches as further evidence of weakness. While prolific in founding new branches, it is alleged that British MNEs overinvested in safe locations. As a contribution to the debate over the performance of British MNEs, this article examines the location of British FDI and assesses the location decision behind inter-war manufacturing investment in production plants.

The Location of British FDI

The absence of large quantitative samples has led to much debate about the geographical distribution of British FDI. Using a sample of 14 MNEs who were among the largest 100 manufacturing firms in 1970 with pre-1914 overseas investments, John Stopford argued that British MNEs followed the path of least resistance, fleeing the competitive developed markets for the protected underdeveloped Empire.[18] In the inter-war period, the follower firms (those without FDIs before 1914) continued to seek out Empire markets, especially the Dominions. Here, British MNEs found a haven of sanity and security in contrast to the inter-war continental and American markets with their cartel arrangements, restrictive government policies and barriers to trade.[19] The pre-1914 pioneers were an exception. Having crossed the threshold of international experience through their pre-1914 FDIs, these pioneers invested in Europe during the interwar years. But the tendency was for British FDI to be concentrated in the Empire, and Stopford explained this concentration by competitive weakness among the 14 MNEs.[20] Industrial retardation in the home market and the failure of British firms to grasp the technological advantages of the 'second' industrial revolution, weakened the competitive ability of British MNEs, restricting their international involvement to the safe Empire markets.

In his comparison of US and UK transnational firms, Chandler echoed Stopford's claims that British MNEs sought safe Empire markets.[21] According to Chandler, managerial failure especially in marketing, restricted British MNEs to safe white Commonwealth markets rather than the more competitive and difficult markets of continental Europe or India. Again, the managerial failure argument which concluded that British MNEs were forced into the protected Empire markets mirrors the older literature on entrepreneurial failure. For example, Hobsbawm argued that, faced with a competitive challenge, British entrepreneurs retreated into a satellite world of formal and informal colonies and Mathias painted a picture of British goods, particularly textiles, seeking 'soft' markets in India, the Far East and the Empire.[22] According to Kirby, British trade sought the line of least resistance in the imperial markets and underdeveloped parts of the world not yet penetrated by foreign competition.[23]

Taking up this theme, Jones accused British multinationals of lacking competitive vigor, repeating the allegation that British MNEs had poor marketing and selling techniques.[24] In a case study which tested whether the Empire was a safe haven, Jones suggested that the poor performance of Cadbury-Fry was due to severe competitive pressure and poor management in Australia and Canada in the 1920s.[25] In his summary of the eight LSE multinational case studies, Jones returned to the issue of competitive vigour arguing that it was not very helpful to view inter-war Empire markets as paths of least resistance.[26] The Commonwealth was not a safe haven; British firms performed poorly both in the competitive developed markets and in the protected Empire markets. But the LSE case studies seem to show a different pattern. Empire markets may have offered little protection for British firms, but the sample of eight firms shows that the British MNEs virtually abandoned the American market (where FDI fell by 75 per cent) and Europe (where the fall in investment was 50 per cent) for the Empire in the inter-war period.[27]

The absence of large quantitative samples has led, then, to much speculation and conjecture, but little hard evidence, about the geographical distribution of British FDI. The database for this study is a sample of 448 pre-1939 manufacturing multinationals. The location of British FDI is measured by the number of plants. There is no adequate data on the conventional measures of FDI, such as sales or profits of plants. Even archival studies rarely provide adequate data on the size of a firm's FDI, and there is no consistent archival data on re-investments. Measuring the number of plants, rather than the value of British FDI, may introduce biases into the location figures, under or overestimating the importance of various markets. However, the number of plants as a proxy for the location of British FDI is unlikely to be improved upon and is consistent with the data used by Stopford, Chandler and Jones.

Using the number of plants, Table 1 shows that developed and underdeveloped Europe took 43 per cent of total British FDI before 1914, outstripping the Empire with 32 per cent of total FDI. Looking at Britain's most important overseas markets in Table 2, Germany and the US attracted more first time investment in plants than Australia and Canada, and France ranked ahead of New Zealand, India and South Africa as a recipient of British FDI. There is no evidence to support Stopford's case that British firms sought a safe haven and gained experience in the Empire before 1914. Nor did pre-1914 MNEs turn to the European markets in the inter-war years as Stopford's small sample implied. Table 3 shows that MNEs which invested in the Empire or the rest of the world pre-1914, invested equally in the Empire, rest of the world or both after 1920. Chandler's contention that British MNEs sold first to the white Commonwealth then the rest of the world also finds little support. British sales branches were as widely spread geographically as British overseas production, and, as Table 2 shows, Germany, France and America attracted sales branches as readily as the Dominions.

TABLE 1
REGIONAL DISTRIBUTION OF BRITISH FDI IN PRODUCTION PLANTS
(per cent)

	Pre-1914	Post-1914
Developed		
Empire	28	41
USA	13	11
Europe	23	18
Other	3	1
Sub-total	67	71
Undeveloped		
Empire	6	11
Europe	20	9
Other	8	9
Sub-Total	34	29

Sources: Database on British pre-1939 multinationals.

Using Table 1 to test the structure of the regional distribution of British FDI, a chi-square test reported no significant difference in the pre- and post-First World War pattern of British investment. However, within the overall pattern of British FDI there were inter-regional shifts. From Table 1 it is clear that there was a move to the Empire markets after 1914, with the shift coming at the expense of European markets. Contrary to the evidence from the eight firms in the LSE study, there was no significant move out of the American market, and the retreat from Europe was from the underdeveloped and not the developed regions of the continent. The stable share of the developed European and American markets, where British MNEs faced serious competition during the inter-war years, suggests that British firms could compete in the world's markets.

The shift of British FDI from underdeveloped Europe to Empire markets does not necessarily reflect any competitive failure on the part of British firms. As shown in Table 4, British MNEs invested across a wide spectrum of product groups and markets through the whole 1870–1939 period. This contrasts sharply with the narrower product range and market penetration by American and European MNEs. European firms concentrated on European markets and on a restrictive range of

TABLE 2

CHOICE OF LOCATION FOR BRITISH PRE-1914 FDI

(number)

	Production Branches					Sales Branches			
	Choice					Choice			
	1st	2nd	3rd	Total of		1st	2nd	3rd	Total of
Germany	19	4	9	30	Australia	13	5	5	23
Australia	7	12	4	27	Germany	15	5	1	23
USA	11	4	3	19	France	10	5	1	18
Canada	10	4	1	18	Canada	8	2	4	16
France	5	0	3	11	S.Africa	6	4	2	12
India	5	1	0	10	USA	9	1	2	12
New Zealand	6	0	1	9	India	4	3	2	11
S.Africa	6	2	1	9	New Zealand	2	0	2	5

Source: Database on British pre-1939 multinationals.

TABLE 3

INTER-WAR INVESTMENT PATTERNS BY PRE-1914 MNEs

(per cent)

Pre-1914 Investment	Inter-war Investment		
	Empire	Rest of the World	Empire and Rest of the World
Empire	31	10	58
Rest of the World	33	17	50

Source: Database on British pre-1939 multinationals.

TABLE 4
PRODUCT GROUP COMPOSITION OF BRITISH FDI
(per cent)

Product	Pre-1914	Post-1914
Food	17	14
Drink	2	2
Chemicals	25	24
Electrical Engineering	9	13
Mechanical Engineering	7	6
Metal Manufacture	6	7
Shipbuilding	1	1
Vehicles	1	3
Metals Goods	1	5
Textiles	15	9
Leather/Fur	1	1
Clothing	1	1
Brick/Clay	3	4
Timber	1	1
Paper/Publishing	3	4
Other Manufacturing	11	8

Source: Database on British pre-1939 multinationals.

products, mostly chemicals, pharmaceuticals and electrical goods; American MNEs, showing a preference for South American countries and Canada, had a comparative advantage in engineering and chemical products.[28] While Table 4 shows no dramatic shifts in the product composition of British FDI, the fall in the share of textiles and the rise in the share of vehicles and electrical engineering after 1914 reflected a competitve awareness of declining and growing product sectors by British MNEs.

The shift towards Empire markets by British MNEs during the inter-war years is not, by itself, evidence of failure. If Empire markets had lower levels of political risk, fewer government restrictions and offered incentives to British firms relative to other markets, a shift towards

Empire signals success; the absence of a shift, on the other hand, would be evidence of failure. Below, I specify a general model of international investment, where location factors are important variables. From this general model I construct an empirical model of the location of British FDI, providing an econometric test of whether the Empire–non-Empire locational choice of British inter-war MNEs suggests failure.

Modelling the Location Decision

Business historians have found the new institutional microeconomic theory of the firm a fruitful approach for analysing the origins and growth of the MNE. MNEs transact internationally to transfer goods and services across national boundaries and to earn quasi-rents from firm-specific assets, including technology, marketing know-how, product differentiation advantages and management skills. If markets worked costlessly, there would be no international firms. In this case, orthodox trade theory, which is really a theory of location, becomes the operative body of knowledge for modelling the geographical spread of investment. However, orthodox trade theory does not admit a problem of management, and is, therefore, unable to distinguish between portfolio and foreign direct investment. But it is hierarchy, or the firm with managers making internal decisions about the allocation of resources, which distinguishes FDI from portfolio investment. Indeed the new micro-institutional theory views the firm as an institution which minimises the costs of gaining information, bargaining and negotiating contracts, and monitoring and enforcing those contracts, in arm's-length markets. These costs of using markets which firms minimise are labelled transaction costs and firms replace markets whenever the transaction costs in the market are greater than the costs of internal firm administration.

Of course, firms are not the only hierarchical organisations which attenuate transaction costs. Cartels, for example, are hierarchical institutions which allocate resources internationally. Moreover, there are a number of governance structures for transacting internationally, such as long term contracts, agencies, franchises and joint ventures, which fall between arm's-length markets and the hierarchical firm. Transaction cost theory is really a general model helping to explain the choice between these alternative institutional arrangements and their location across national frontiers.

In fact, the choice of institutional arrangements for transacting internationally and the location of the institution is made simultaneously. For analytical purposes I assume that the choice of the firm as the transactional mode has already been made and concentrate here on location factors. I have discussed the choice of institutional form elsewhere, and sketch the choice of form only briefly before turning to the derivation of a model for the location of the FDI.[29]

Historically, British MNEs first exported to foreign markets, sometimes using merchant houses, then developed an agency system, before making their first FDI in the form of a sales branch which was subsequently replaced by a production plant.[30] It is costly to monitor and enforce agency arrangements, especially when there is a high volume of transactions and the need for idiosyncratic investment (such as credit facilities, repair shops and advertising) by the agent and the principal. Agents can cheat principals by providing a low level of sales effort or by blowing the principal's reputation through poor sales service, repair or credit facilities. When the principal invests in idiosyncratic capital, such as brand name advertising, then poor service by an agent depreciates the principal's investment. Clearly, the greater the volume of sales, the more costly an indifferent sales effort and poor level of service by agents. The transaction costs related to opportunistic agents, who maximise their welfare at the expense of the principal, are attenuated when sales branches replace agencies.

The shift from sales branches to production plants can also be understood in transaction cost terms.[31] Two types of transaction costs are internalised in production branches: the rents from production-based knowledge which are not easily codified and patented and scope economies related to managing at a distance. Uncoded and unpatented production-based knowledge have public good characteristics which means they cannot be costly traded in arm's-length markets. The MNE is an institution which allows such knowledge to be transferred internationally. Scope economies arise when the costs of joint production, particularly related to management knowledge, are less within a single international firm located in two or more different countries than the costs of producing in separate plants in each country. Transaction cost factors, then, are important elements in understanding the choice of institutional form. Of course, the form of institution is determined by other factors, such as production costs, but no model of FDI is complete without the specification of transaction costs. Assuming that the choice of sales branch or production plant has been reached, this paper models the location of inter-war British FDI.

Business historians have been aware of locational factors in the growth of the MNE. Franko pointed to the mismatch between continental borders and plentiful raw materials to explain the vertical integration of continental Euroean MNEs into oil, copper, iron ore and bauxite.[32] In a study of eight cases of investment in the US before 1914, Buckley and Roberts concluded that the imposition of new tariffs was a common motive for making a FDI.[33] Tariffs have been identified by company historians as the most important factor (and sometimes as the exclusive factor) in a firm's FDI decision. For example, Chandler thought that the reason British family firms built overseas plants was tariffs, whether in the United States, the Continent or the Commonwealth.[34] In the LSE case studies, Jones rejected Chandler's view that all British strategies by British firms were defensive rather than aggressive.[35] Jones found that of the 24 pre-1914 decisions to establish an overseas branch, 42 per cent were due to host market size and 29 per cent to tariffs or host government pressure, while the percentages were 35 per cent and 38 per cent for the 34 inter-war investment decisions.[36] In a recent study of British FDI between 1870 and 1983, Dunning and Archer focused on high income foreign markets and the importance of tariff restrictions for the timing of the investment decision.[37] Perhaps the best attempt to integrate home and host country factors into an explanation of FDI is Wilkins' survey of similarities and differences between North American and European multinationals.[38] British MNEs, Wilkins argued, were encouraged to invest in the Empire due to a familiar political infrastructure which reduced uncertainty and to obtain raw material supplies by integrating backwards.

These qualitative approaches to the location of British FDI fail to provide a measure of the relative importance of locational factors. While some locational factors were held to be more important than others, this relative importance was usually posited rather than tested. The one exception was the eight case studies collected by the LSE group when firm histories were used to discover the reason for the FDI decision. From a close reading of firm histories and archival work, I consider an expanded range of factors for 176 British multinationals to test econometrically the inter-war location decision. These location variables enter the model in an *ad hoc* fashion as opposed to being modelled directly. Of course, this is also true of implicit models employed by business historians, and springs in large part from the absence of a theory of location for FDI.

Generally, the location decision depends on host country variables, costs related to distance and production costs. Host country variables include income per head, tariffs, government policy, political risk, language and the types of host country economic and social institutions. Production costs which depend on wage, input and energy costs, labour productivity, tax concessions, import protection and bounty payments, are, in part, industry specific. Costs related to distance are transport costs and costs of organising and controlling a branch a long way from head office. Unfortunately, observations on many of the above variables, such as income per head, labour productivity and wage costs, do not exist for all 58 countries which received British FDI during the inter-war years. Further, several variables, such as the impact of distance on home office control, have no obvious direct measure and are difficult to proxy. However, it is possible to construct a number of important locational variables which allows a model of the Empire–non-Empire choice of FDI to be tested. The dependent variable is a binary, taking on the value 1 if the firm invested mainly in the Empire between 1919 and 1939, and 0 otherwise.

Host market locational factors are represented by PSYCHIC, GOVT and TARIFF. PSYCHIC is psychic proximity which encourages the flow of goods between markets. It depends on the similarities in the level of development between home and host country, including education, language, culture, customs and legal and commerical systems.[39] PSYCHIC was proxied by whether English was the natural language of the host country. Of course, other proxies, such as the presence of a parliamentary system of government or an English common law legal system, might have been used in place of language, but language provides an unambiguous measure which captures the cultural similarities between countries.

GOVT, or government, measures the FDI incentives which host governments provide to MNEs. These can take many forms, including protection from imports, government sponsorship of FDI or threats to open negotiations with competitors. Based on archive material and business histories, it was possible to identify for each firm whether government played an important role in encouraging FDI. Similarly, it was possible to identify from the same sources whether tariffs were a barrier to FDI, allowing TARIFF to be specified for each firm. Finally, access to raw materials has been seen by business historians as an important motivation for FDI. Using firm histories and archival material, RAW measured for each firm whether FDI was motivated by the search for raw materials. All four of these variables are dichotomous. The hypothesised signs of the variables for firms investing in the Empire are positive for PSYCHIC, GOVT and RAW and negative for TARIFF.

Production costs, including distribution and marketing costs, are likely to be industry specific. These were proxied by a binary based on the two digit SIC, with FOOD/DRINK, CHEMICAL, and ENGINEER directly entering the model and all other product groups subsumed in the constant. We expect that the sign on FOOD to be negative, while the sign of the other product groups to be positive.

Finally, the model tries to capture the impact of distance through the specification of two continuous firm-specific variables related to age, AGE, and span of the enterprise, DIVER. It is hypothesised that the older the firm, the better it is at managing at a distance, therefore, I expect the sign of AGE to be positive. Also the more diversified the firm, measured by the number of different two digit SIC products the firm produces, the more complex its internal structure is likely to be and the more efficient its control mechanisms. The expected sign of DIVER is positive.

Since each firm faced the binary choice of investing in the Empire or in the non-Empire, limited-dependent or qualitative choice models provide an appropriate characterisation of the investment decision. For firm i, given the matrix of explanatory variables denoted X_i, we assume the probability of investing in a Empire, P_i, can be described by the logistic function.

$$P_i = \frac{1}{1 + \exp(-\beta X)} \qquad -\infty < \beta X < \infty \qquad (1)$$

where β are the coefficients to be estimated. Only one observation is available for each firm, therefore P_i must be estimated by maximum likelihood techniques rather than by the usual method of sample proportions. For T observations, the likelihood function is:

$$\ell = \prod_{i-1}^{T} P_i^{y_i} (1-P_i)^{1-y_i} \quad (2)$$

where

$$y_i = \begin{cases} 1 \text{ with a probability } P_i \\ 0 \text{ with a probability } 1-P_i \end{cases}$$

which is estimated by the Newton-Raphson iterative procedure for maximising nonlinear objective functions.[40]

The econometric results in Table 5 suggest that the inter-war decision by British MNEs to invest in the Empire was rational. From Model 1, the probability of investing in the Empire increased with PSYCHIC and GOVT. Both coefficients were positive and highly significant, confirming our *a priori* hypothesis that psychic proximity and government incentives increased the likelihood of British firms investing in Empire markets. The negative (and significant) coefficient on TARIFF, discouraged British MNEs from investing in the Empire. The search for raw inputs into the production process increased the probability of investing in the Empire, but the coefficient was not significant. The SIC product classifications were used to proxy production costs; the sign on CHEMICAL and ENGINEER were positive, but neither coefficient was significant, while FOOD/DRINK had the predicted negative sign, and was significant at the 90 per cent level. Both AGE and DIVER were used to proxy the costs of doing business at a distance, and while both had the correct signs only AGE was significant. In so far as AGE and DIVER capture the more complex internal structures and experience of doing business, both increase the likelihood of investing in the Empire.

DIVER and RAW are correlated in Model 1. This can be seen in the dramatic change in the value of the DIVER coefficient in Model 2 and the RAW coefficient in Model 3. In spite of multicollinearity between RAW and DIVER, both variables are at work in the FDI decision, and the preferred model remains Model 1. All the other variables are stable across the three models. In all three models the log likelihood chi-square statistic for the logit equations allow the null model, with all coefficients equal to zero, to be rejected. Overall, the host country variables are the most important in determining the likelihood that British MNEs invested in Empire markets in the inter-war years, but distance and production costs also were significant in the invest-ment decision. Clearly, the decision to invest in the Empire was economically rational.

TABLE 5
LOGIT EQUATIONS FOR EMPIRE–NON-EMPIRE LOCATION DECISION

	Model 1	Model 2	Model 3
AGE	0.014	0.014	0.013
	(2.570)	(2.636)	(2.487)
DIVER	0.743	1.179	
	(1.128)	(2.281)	
RAW	0.789		1.221
	(1.150)		(2.288)
FOOD/DRINK	-1.027	-0.983	-1.098
	(-1.735)	(-1.759)	(-1.933)
CHEMICAL	0.262		
	(0.514)		
ENGINEER	0.185)		
	(0.366)		
TARIFF	-0.948	-0.897	-0.846
	(-2.009)	(-1.957)	(-1.868)
PSYCHIC	3.306	3.213	3.256
	(5.380)	(5.350)	(5.373)
GOVT	2.096	2.023	2.089
	(3.513)	(3.429)	(3.536)
CONSTANT	0.055	0.181	0.199
	(0.121)	(0.477)	(0.518)
x^2	67.348	65.693	65.787
d.f.	9	6	6
No. of cases	176	176	176

Note: Asympotic t ratios in parentheses.

Case Study Evidence

The econometric evidence suggests that during the inter-war years British MNEs sought out Empire markets because they provided locational advantages over the rest of the world. This implies no failure or competitive weakness on the part of British MNEs. Case study evidence provides ample support for these empirical conclusions. Nationalism, the pressure by both governments and consumers for production branches rather than an export sales organisation, became an increasingly important non-tariff barrier in the post-1918 international economy. In a 1919 survey of its international commitments, Babcock acknowledged nationalist pressure not only in Italy, but also Canada and Australia, which encouraged the firm to establish branch plants in all three countries in the early 1920s.[41] Dunlop's 1936 investment in India was a response, in part, to nationalism, and nationalism led Brunner Mond in the 1920s to create a local identity by establishing production branches.[42] Not only did host country firms use their indigenous nationality as a selling weapon against MNE branch sales offices, but governments encouraged investment in production to gain technology and 'self-sufficiency'. Government encouragement was particularly strong in the Empire. ICI believed that the Australian government through its tariff structure had a self-sufficiency policy during the 1930s and, threatened with State and Federal government inducements to other chemical firms, ICI entered into a joint venture with local Australian interests.[43] Federal government 'inducement' to establish production is illustrated by Prime Minister Hughes' threat in 1920 to encourage American boiler makers to invest in Australia, unless Babcock established a manufacturing subsidiary.[44] The Prime Minister also promised Babcock that no duties would be levelled on certain components required by the firm. The written no duty agreement with Babcock, lodged with the Tariff Board, was used to defeat new tariffs on boiler parts before the 1934–35 Tariff Board Enquiry on boilers and remained a binding agreement as late as the 1967 Tariff Board Enquiries. A similar promise, this time of tariff protection against imports, induced British Insulated Cables to help establish a metal manufacturing capability in Australia in 1919.[45]

Australia provides an ideal case study of MNE investment behaviour under the most severe tariff barriers and self-sufficiency policy experienced by British MNEs in the Empire. While Empire restrictions restricted British FDI. Britain also faced tariff and non-tariff barriers from the rest of the world. While Dunlop was aware of nationalism in Germany before 1933, Nazi economic policy imposed legal restrictive non-trade barriers including the forced purchase of locally-made imports, membership in an official price cartel, and restrictions on imported rubber and cotton.[46] All dividends above six per cent had to be invested in German bonds and remittances of profits and dividends were effectively stopped. In 1936 Dunlop was forced to reinvest in Germany in order 'to maintain friendly relations with the Government'.[47] Babcock and Courtaulds faced similar exchange controls on profits and restrictions in dividend remittances from Germany after 1935. The cumulative impact of German economic policy was effectively to free Babcock's German subsidiary from parental control.[48] In 1920 Babcock (Germany) had tried to export boilers outside the 'German Empire' in direct competition with English Babcock and in violation of the 1908 contract limiting the territorial sales of the German branch. Babcock forced the Germany subsidiary to abandon all third market sales. After 1933, with the German State controlling export orders and prices of Babcock (Germany), the English parent conceded that territorial sales restrictions could not be enforced, sanctioning competition between Babcock and its German subsidiary in third markets. Confronted with nationalist pressures in Japan, Dunlop tried unsuccessfully to take on minority local equity interests in 1931 and majority local control in 1937.[49] Also in Japan, Babcock tried to negotiate a local minority partnership with Mitsui between 1927 and 1930, admitting that Babcock 'could not obtain a proper share of the (Japanese) market for boilers under British control'.[50] In 1939 a London director negotiated the sale of a majority share holding in Babcock (Japan) to Mitsui at less than its market value, only to be prohibited from repatriating the profits.

Some British firms, such as Cadbury, which refused to enter the German market and Lewis Berger which 'dispersed their interests away from Europe' in the 1930s, rejected non-Empire markets in the inter-war period.[51] This is reflected more generally in the significant redirection of British investment away from Germany and Japan. As Table 2 shows, before 1914 Germany ranked as Britain's market of first choice for making FDIs, while in the inter-war years Germany fell to eighth place as the first choice of British investment. Two thirds of all British post-1918 investment in Germany occurred before 1933. While FDI fell in Germany and Japan, less risky forms of overseas involvement increased with a doubling of licensing agreements in those countries.

Investment barriers were not restricted to Fascist regimes. After 1932 Eire's policy of self-sufficiency in basic consumer goods was enforced through tariffs and import controls.[52] The introduction of tariffs in 1932 and quotas in 1934 induced John Halliday, John Rawson, J.H. Woodington, E. Donaghy & Son, Toone & Son and Padmore & Barnes to begin shoe production in the Irish Free State.[53] In 1936 the Government forced shoe-making firms to establish plants outside Dublin and in 1938 all new FDI was effectively prohibited. Due to lack of management expertise, C. & J. Clark did not enter the Irish market in the early 1930s. As sales dropped from £20,000 in 1930 to only £4,000 in 1938, Clarks entered a complex licensing arrangement with Halliday, which produced shoes to Clarks' design which were then marketed through a Clark controlled sales branch.[54]

Finally, there is evidence that Empire markets were advantaged by psychic proximity relative to the rest of the world. In a 1928 survey of its Brussels branch, Babcock reported that 'distance, language and customs' required a more complete organisation in Belgium than at home.[55] In Germany, Japan and Italy, the ideology, institutions and practices of Fascism created high psychic costs. Political risk was greater outside than inside the Empire. After the 1919 decision to invest in Italy, Babcock delayed investing until 1925 when the 'political situation and industrial unrest stabilised'.[56] In China, Babcock reported that its business was paralysed due to political conditions in 1926 and Callender Cables shut its China office due to internal disorder in 1936.[57] Babcock delegated decision-making power to individuals in Spain to protect the company's assets during the Spanish Civil War.[58] Cadbury's plans for a FDI in Burk & Braun of Germany, was stopped, according to Jones, by worries over the 'morality of business in Germany'.[59] Psychic distance was reflected in Cadbury's request, and Burk & Braun's refusal, to 'keep accounts and render returns on the English standard'.[60]

Conclusions

While pre-1939 British FDI was world-wide, there were important regional concentrations. British MNEs increasingly directed their FDI towards the industrialised countries and away from the under-developed parts of the international economy. Within Europe, for example, British FDI shifted from the undeveloped countries to developed Europe. Authors who have used very small samples of the largest MNEs have tended to distort the location, and changes in the location, of British FDI resulting in misleading interpretations about the competitive behaviour of British MNEs. The new quantitative evidence reported here suggests that British MNEs were competitive before 1914, directing 40 per cent of their investments to developed countries, especially continental Europe and the United States. For example, Germany and the United States were the first and second choice as destinations of FDI by British MNEs.

While inter-war FDI was directed towards the Empire, this is not, by itself, evidence that British firms sought a safe haven or that British selling methods or techniques were inefficient. A logit model of locational choice between the Empire and the rest of the world showed that Empire markets offered host economy advantages in terms of psychic proximity, government encouragement and raw material advantages over non-Empire markets. Locational advantages explain the decision by British MNEs to shift their investments towards the Empire after 1918. These econometric and empirical results, based on a large quantitative sample, were supplemented by case studies evidence. The inter-war problems faced by the management of Babcock, C. & J. Clark, Callender Cable, British Insulated Cable, Dunlop and Cadbury in both Empire and non-Empire markets illustrated the importance of psychic proximity, government, tariffs and nationalism in directing the location of inter-war FDI towards the Empire. Both the case study and quantitative evidence suggests that British managers reacted rationally to economic factors, providing no evidence that FDI was directed to the wrong markets or to avoid competition.

University of New South Wales

NOTES

1. S. Nicholas, 'British Multinational Investment Before 1939', *Journal of European Economic History*, Vol.XI, No.3 (1982).
2. S. Nicholas, 'Agency Contracts, Transactional Modes and the Transition to Foreign Direct Investment by British Manufacturing Multinational Before 1939', *Journal of Economic History*, Vol.XLIII, No.3 (1983); S. Nicholas, 'The Theory of Multinational Enterprise as a Transactional Mode', in P. Hertner and G. Jones (eds.), *Multinationals: Theory and History* (Aldershot, 1986); G. Jones, 'Multinational Chocolate: Cadbury Overseas, 1918–1939', *Business History*, Vol. XXVII, No.1 (1984); G. Jones, 'The Gramophone Company: An Anglo-American Multinational, 1898–1931', *Business History Review*, Vol.59, No.1 (1985); G. Jones, 'The Growth and Performance of British Multinational Firms Before 1939: The Case of Dunlop', *Economic History Review*, Vol.XXXVII, No.1 (1984); G. Jones (ed.), *British Multinationals: Origins, Management and Performance* (Aldershot, 1986); M. Wilkins, 'The History of European Multinationals: A New Look', *The Journal of European Economic History*, Vol.15, No.3 (1986).
3. Attempts to aggregate case studies have been undertaken by S. Nicholas, 'Agency Contracts'; M. Casson, 'Contractual Arrangements for Technology Transfer – New Evidence from Business History', *Business History*, Vol.XXVII, No.4 (1987).
4. For a more detailed discussion see D. Hutchinson and S. Nicholas, 'Modelling the Growth Strategies of British Firms', *Business History*, Vol.XXIX, No.4 (Special Issue; 1987); Jones, *British Multinationals*.
5. G. Jones, 'The Performance of British Multinational Enterprise 1890–1945', in Hertner and Jones (eds.), *Multinationals*, pp.97–104.
6. Jones, *British Multinationals*.
7. A. Chandler, 'The Growth of the Transnational Industrial Firm in the United States and United Kingdom: A Comparative Analysis', *Economic History Review*, Vol. XXXIII, No.3 (1980).
8. G. Jones, 'Origins, Management and Performance', in Jones (ed.), *British Multinationals*, pp.13–20.
9. R. Church, 'Family Firms and Managerial Capitalism: The Case of the International Motor Industry', *Business History*, Vol.XXVII, No.2 (1980).
10. Wilkins, 'European Multinationals', pp.494–5.
11. L. Hannah, *The Rise of the Corporate Economy* (London, 1983), pp.70–89.
12. Chandler, 'Transnational', pp.401–9; Jones, 'Performance', pp.106–7.
13. D. Aldcroft, 'The Entrepreneur and the British Economy, 1870–1914', *Economic History Review*, Vol.XII, No.1 (1964), p.125.
14. D. Landes, *The Unbound Prometheus* (Cambridge, 1969), p.337.
15. M. Kirby, *The Decline of British Economic Power* (London, 1981), p.8; W. Lewis, *Growth and Fluctuations, 1870–1913* (London, 1978), pp.121–2.
16. P. Payne, *British Entrepreneurship in the Nineteenth Century* (London, 1974),

pp.53–4.
17. S. Nicholas, 'The Overseas Marketing Performance of British Industry, 1870–1914', *Economic History Review*, Vol.XXXVII, No.4 (1984).
18. J. Stopford, 'Origins of British-Based Multinational Manufacturing Enterprises', *Business History Review*, Vol.XLVIII, No.3 (1974), p.314. For a dissenting view see R. Davenport-Hines (ed.), *Markets and Bagmen: Studies in the History of Marketing and British Industrial Performances 1830–1939* (Aldershot, 1986).
19. Ibid., p.327.
20. Ibid., pp.311–12.
21. Chandler, 'Transnational', pp.401–9.
22. E. Hobsbawm, *Industry and Empire* (Harmondsworth, 1968), p.191; P. Mathias, *The First Industrial Nation* (London, 1969), pp.413–14.
23. Kirby, *Decline*, p.7.
24. Jones, 'Performance', pp.106–7.
25. Jones, 'Multinational Chocolate', pp.64, 74.
26. Jones, 'Origins, Management', pp.16–18.
27. Ibid., p.17.
28. L. Franko, *The European Multinationals* (London, 1977), p.77; Jones, 'Origins, Management', pp.4–5; M. Wilkins, *The Emergence of Multinational Enterprise* (Cambridge, MA, 1970), pp.199–217.
29. See S. Nicholas, 'Transactional Mode', pp.64–79; S. Nicholas, 'Multinationals, Transaction Costs and Choice of Institutional Firm', *University of Reading Discussion Paper in International Business*, No.99 (1986).
30. Nicholas, 'Multinational Investment', pp.620–21.
31. See S. Nicholas, 'The Expansion of British Multinational Firms: Testing for Managerial Failure, 1870–1939', in J. Foreman-Peck, (ed.), *Reinterpreting the Nineteenth Century British Economy: Essays in Quantitative Economic History* (forthcoming, Cambridge, 1989).
32. Franko, *European Multinationals*, pp.27–8.
33. P. Buckley and B. Roberts, *European Direct Investment in the USA Before World War I* (London, 1982), pp.44, 67, 87, 91–2.
34. Chandler, 'Transnationals', p.401.
35. Jones, 'Origins, Management', p.8.
36. Ibid.
37. J. Dunning and H. Archer, 'The Electric Paradigm and the Growth of U.K. Multinational Enterprise 1870–1983', *University of Reading Discussion Paper in International Business* No.109, pp.25–33.
38. M. Wilkins, 'European and North American Multinationals, 1870–1914: Comparisons and Contrasts', *Business History*, Vol. XXX, No. 1 (1988), pp.8–45.
39. J. Dunning, *International Production and the Multinational Enterprise* (London, 1981), p.102.
40. T.B. Formby et. al., *Advanced Econometric Methods* (New York, 1984); G. Judge et al., *The Theory and Practice of Econometrics* (New York, 1980).
41. *Babcock Minute Book*, 14 May 1919.
42. G. Jones, *British Multinationals*, p.29; W. Reader, *Imperial Chemical Industries*, Vol.1 (London, 1970), p.337.
43. Ibid., Vol.2, pp.267–70.
44. C. Bellamy, *Memoirs of Babcock Australia* (private typescript), pp.20–21.
45. *British Insulated Cables Minute Book*.
46. Jones, 'Dunlop', p.49.
47. Ibid.
48. Babcock, 'Series of Letters Over Territory, 1919–1920', uncatalogued; 'German File', uncatalogued.
49. Jones, 'Dunlop', p.45.
50. *Babcock Minute Book*, 17 May 1939; 3 Aug. 1939.
51. Jones, 'Multinational Chocolate', p.67.
52. Sixty per cent of British FDI in Eire occurred after 1932.

53. J. Press, *Irish Footwear Industry History* (manuscript 1984, Clark Archives), pp.36–42.
54. C. & J. Clark, *Foreign Trade: Ireland*, Box H2/25; *Memo for Managers*, 13 July 1937, Box H2/25.
55. Babcock, *The Circulator* July 1928, pp.30–31.
56. *Babcock Minute Book*, 7 Jan. 1931; *China Memorandum*, 14 July 1936.
57. Babcock, *China Memorandum*, 14 July 1936.
58. *Babcock Executive and Financial Committee Minute Book*, 23 Feb. 1932.
59. Jones, 'Multinational Chocolate', p.67.
60. Ibid.

INDEX

Printed in the United States
by Baker & Taylor Publisher Services